ONE WORLD

Civic, Social and Political Education for
JUNIOR CERTIFICATE

EDCO

Deirdre Murphy   Jim Ryan

Contents

Section 1   Welcome to CSPE 1

Section 2   **Rights and Responsibilities** 13

2.1 The Individual's Rights and Responsibilities 13

2.2 Rights and Responsibilities in the Community 27

2.3 Ireland: The Citizen's Rights and Responsibilities 31

2.4 Rights and Responsibilities: An International View 35

Section 3   **Human Dignity** 41

3.1 Human Dignity and the Individual 41

3.2 Our Community 51

3.3 The State's Role in Upholding Human Dignity 59

3.4 An International Case Study in Human Dignity: Child Labour 61

Section 4   **Stewardship** 69

4.1 The Individual as steward of the planet 69

4.2 Stewardship in the community 73

4.3 National Issues in Stewardship 77

4.4 Stewardship – The International Connection 80

Section 5   **Democracy** 88

5.1 What is democracy? 88

5.2 Our Democratic Community 92

5.3 Ireland – A Democratic State 94

5.4 Democracy: International Case Studies 110

Section 6   **Law** 115

6.1 Citizenship and the law 115

6.2 Law at the local level 120

6.3 Irish Law – Some Key Aspects 124

6.4 Law – An International Dimension 134

Section 7   **Development** 139

7.1 Development and the individual 139

7.2 Community Development 143

7.3 Regional Development in Ireland 150

7.4 World Development Issues 153

Section 8   **Interdependence** 161

8.1 No-one is an Island 161

8.2 Cooperation in the Community 164

8.3 Interdependence – Ireland, The European Union and the Council of Ministers 168

8.4 Our International Connections 177

Section 9   **Assessment** 189

The Report on the Action Project – (RAP) 190

The Coursework Assessment Book – (CWAB) 194

The Written Examination 198

Welcome to CSPE

Civic, Social and Political Education – **CSPE** – is a course of study that prepares young people for **active citizenship**. The course is based on **human rights** and **social responsibilities**. Over the next three years you will explore many issues related to CSPE. These issues are all around you – on the television, in newspapers and magazines – and are evident in the many communities to which you belong.

Look at the newspaper headlines below. These will give you a flavour of some of the issues central to CSPE.

Residents Kick Up Stink Over Proposed Dump

€3 BILLION PLEDGED TO THE DEVELOPING WORLD

Dáil proposes new Citizenship Laws

TIDY TOWNS WINNER TO BE ANNOUNCED TOMORROW

Refugee Injured in Racial Attack

SUPERMARKET INTRODUCES FAIRTRADE PRODUCE

LOW TURN-OUT PREDICTED IN BY-ELECTION

Homeless accommodation needed in Cork

TRAVELLER AWARDED €3000 IN DISCRIMINATION CASE

WORKERS DEMAND THEIR RIGHTS

What is Citizenship?

Being a citizen involves **belonging** to a **community**. You belong to many communities – family, school, your locality, the community of Ireland and the wider global community.

CSPE aims to prepare young people for **active citizenship**. Being an active citizen means:

- Being aware of your rights
- Acting responsibly
- Getting involved in the communities you belong to
- Influencing decisions that affect you
- Caring for others in your community.

Below are some examples of active citizens.

 Anne is a member of Neighbourhood Watch. She reports any suspicious activity and incidences of crime to the local Garda.

 Anthony manages the local football team. He trains the team twice a week in the park.

 Tom organises the annual clean-up of the local river.

 Mary volunteers in the local charity shop. She organises clothing collections every month.

 Betty gets the shopping for her elderly neighbour every week.

 Barry and Lucy exercise their right to vote on election day.

 Mark is a member of the student council. He represents the interests of his fellow students.

 Sean organised a petition against the closure of the local post office.

 Sophie is a member of the youth section of a political party. She is interested in politics and how government policies affect her community.

Look at the photos below. They show famous active citizens from Ireland and abroad. How many do you know about? Why are they considered active citizens?

→ **Mary Robinson**   → **Adi Roche**   → **John O'Shea**   → **Bono**

→ **Barack Obama**   → **Bob Geldof**   → **Bishop Desmond Tutu**   → **Aung San Suu Kyi**

Over the next three years you will develop the knowledge and skills that will enable you to become an active citizen. It is important, therefore, that you learn in an active way. Throughout this textbook there are many activities that will help you to develop these skills.

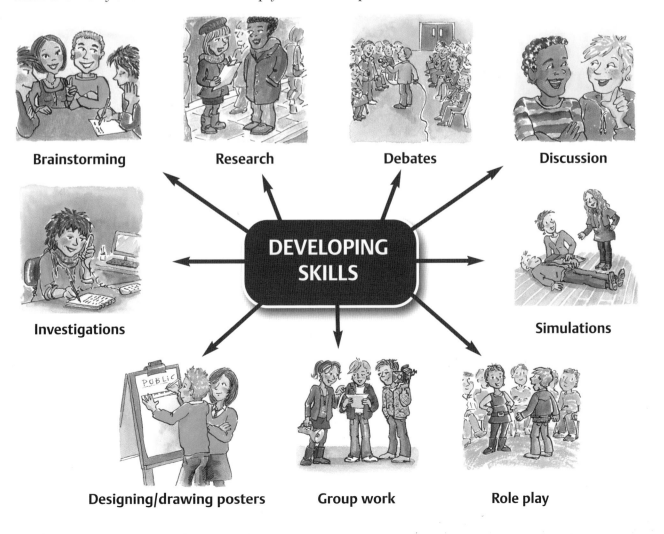

Brainstorming   **Research**   **Debates**   **Discussion**

Investigations

DEVELOPING SKILLS

Simulations

Designing/drawing posters   **Group work**   **Role play**

Seven Concepts – Four Units

The CSPE course is based around seven ideas. These are called **concepts**. The seven concepts which the CSPE course is built upon are:

CONCEPT 1
Rights and Responsibilities

CONCEPT 7
Interdependence

CONCEPT 2
Human Dignity

CONCEPT 6
Development

CONCEPT 3
Stewardship

CONCEPT 5
Law

CONCEPT 4
Democracy

Concept 1

Rights and Responsibilities

Every human being is entitled to basic human rights. These rights are of a civic, social, cultural, economic and political nature. You will learn about these rights and the need for us to safeguard them. You will also learn that each of us has responsibilities towards other human beings in our actions.

Concept 2

Human Dignity

Every individual has the right to live his or her life with dignity and be treated with respect. If individuals are denied certain needs and rights, they can experience a loss of human dignity. There are many individuals and groups in society that experience a lack of human dignity on a daily basis. It is important that each one of us respects and values every person, no matter how different from us they are.

Concept 3

Stewardship

We are temporary owners or stewards of the Earth. It is important that we look after our planet responsibly and ensure that our vital natural resources are safeguarded for future generations. You will learn the importance of acting responsibly when it comes to caring for our planet. Acting irresponsibly can damage it for future generations.

Concept 4

Democracy

Democracy is a form of government whereby citizens elect people to represent them and make decisions on their behalf. Through your study of CSPE you will explore how democratic governments operate. You will also discover how you have the power to bring about change by actively participating in democratic society.

Concept 5

Law

Rules and laws are necessary if the rights of individuals are to be protected and promoted. In this section you will explore why we have laws, how they are made and upheld, and what happens when an individual 'breaks' the law. You will learn about the law in Ireland and in other countries.

Concept 6

Development

Local, national and international communities are in a constant state of change. This change can have profound effects on individuals and communities at local, national and international levels. Although most development is planned and aims to improve the lives of individuals, it can sometimes have a negative impact.

Concept 7

Interdependence

We are all connected or linked to each other in some way at individual, local, national and global levels. We are linked to different countries and people by the food we eat, the clothes we wear and the things we use. Interdependence is a word to describe these linkages. Our actions and the decisions we make in our own country may have an effect on individuals and communities in different countries. There is a responsibility on us all to ensure that these effects are positive rather than negative.

You will find that many of these concepts have common themes with each other and that they may overlap at times.

CSPE Units

The CSPE course is divided up into four areas of study.
These are called **units**.

The four units are:

1 The Individual   **2 The Community**   **3 The State (Ireland)**   **4 The Wider World**

This textbook looks at each of the seven concepts from these four areas of study.

Assessment – An Overview

Like most other subjects on the Junior Certificate Course, CSPE is examined at the end of your three years of study. Assessment of CSPE is carried out in two ways:

Submission of either:	
1. A Report on an Action Project (RAP) OR A Course Work Assessment Book (CWAB)	**60%**
2. A written terminal examination	**40%**

There is a more detailed discussion on Assessment in Section 9.

Taking Action – Action Projects

Over the next three years you will learn how to carry out an **action project**. You have probably done many projects in school where you had to find out information on various topics and present your findings in a folder or scrap book. This is **not** an action project. An action project, as the name suggests, involves **you**, the student, **taking action** on some issue you feel strongly about. However, this issue must be based on one of the seven CSPE concepts we mentioned earlier. Some examples of action projects include:

Writing a Class Charter of Rights and Responsibilities

Presenting a drama

Fundraising

Inviting guest speakers

Holding an Awareness Day in your school

Letter-writing campaigns

Lobbying politicians

Holding mock elections

Organising a petition

Making presentations

Publishing an information booklet

Supervising a recycling campaign

Doing surveys/ questionnaires

Tree-planting

Visits

> **REMEMBER! Your action project must link into one or more of the seven key concepts, otherwise it will be invalid!**

Doing the Action Project – 6 Stages

The six stages involved in carrying out an action project are:

1 Find an issue ➡ 2 Form teams/ committees ➡ 3 Plan committee tasks ➡ 4 Do the action! ➡ 5 Evaluate the action ➡ 6 Report the action

1. Find an Issue

Finding an issue you want to take action on can often be difficult. As a rule of thumb, you should choose an issue that genuinely interests the class and one that you all feel strongly about. Action projects usually arise when:

- You want to find out more about an issue
- You want to do something about an issue
- You feel strongly about a school/local/topical issue
- You want to raise money for a particular organisation/cause
- You want to focus on or celebrate a designated day.

The following calendar features some of the most important designated days. You may want to mark or celebrate one of these days in your school or community as part of your action project.

DESIGNATED DAYS

1st January	World Peace Day
25th January	Martin Luther King Day
March	Fairtrade Fortnight
March	National Tree Week
8th March	International Women's Day
21st March	International Day for the Elimination of Racial Discrimination
22nd March	World Day for Water
April	Telethon
22nd April	Earth Day
1st May	World Labour Day
9th May	Europe Day
15th May	International Day of Families
5th June	World Environment Day
September (3rd week)	Energy Awareness Week
20th September	International Day of Peace
1st October	International Day for the Elderly
16th October	World Food Day
17th October	International Day for the Eradication of Poverty
24th October	United Nations Day
November (3rd week)	One World Week
20th November	Universal Children's Day
3rd December	International Day of the Disabled
10th December	International Human Rights Day

2. Form Teams/Committees

If you are doing a class action project it is important that everybody has a job to do. With this in mind, the class should be divided into teams or committees, each with its own essential job to do. For example, if the action project involves a guest speaker the class could be divided into committees as follows:

1 Permission Committee
2 Contact/Briefing Committee
3 Room Committee
4 Finance Committee
5 Public Relations Committee
6 Questions Committee
7 Welcome Committee
8 Thank You Committee.

3. Plan Committee Tasks

Now that the committees are organised, it is important to note the responsibilities of each one. Every member of the committee should have a role to play. It is vital that each committee keeps a record or log of its progress. A good idea is to use a planning sheet similar to the one below.

ACTION: Guest Speaker
COMMITTEE: Room Committee

DATE	TASK	THINGS TO DO	WHO
24 January	Get equipment organised	Get overhead projector Get flip chart off science teacher	Sean Anne
25 January (after school)	Organise seating plan	Place chairs in a semi-circle	Kim John
25 January (after school)	Clean and tidy classroom	Sweep floor Tidy bookshelves	David Amy
26 January Guest Speaker arrives	Get glass of water for speaker	Get a jug of water from the water cooler and a glass from the staff room	Niall

It is also important that you keep a record of the role that you played as part of the action project. Have your own action plan. It would be a good idea if you recorded your action plan on a sheet similar to the one below.

MY ACTION PLAN: Room Committee

DATE	WHAT DO I NEED	WHERE / HOW DO I GET IT	CAN ANYONE HELP?
25 January	Chairs, tables	From CSPE room and extra chairs from library	Caretaker Other students

4. Do the Action!
Remember! Your action must:
- Be based on one or more of the seven key concepts
- Be from a human rights/social responsibilities perspective
- Involve genuine action, not just research
- Communicate with other people or communities
- Involve all members of the class if it is a class action project.

5. Evaluate the Action
When the action has been completed, there are a number of questions that need to be answered:
- Was the action a success?
- Would you do anything differently? What and why?
- What have you learned?
- What skills have you used/developed?
- What are your thoughts now on that issue?

6. Report the Action
You must now decide how you are going to report on your action. This can be done by writing a **Report on an Action Project** (**RAP**) or by completing a **Course Work Assessment Book** (**CWAB**). See section 9 for more details on this.

Development of Skills
Being an active citizen means having the skills to participate fully in society. Through your study of CSPE and by carrying out action projects, you will develop some of the following:
1 Identification/Awareness skills
2 Analysis/Evaluation skills
3 Communication skills
4 Action skills.

1. Identification/Awareness Skills
These skills enable you to access and acquire **information**. These skills include:

✔ **Emailing Skills**   ✔ **Internet Skills**   ✔ **Interviewing Skills**

✔ **Letter-Writing Skills**   ✔ **Questioning Skills**   ✔ **Surveying Skills**

✔ **Telephone Skills**

2. Analysis/Evaluation Skills

These skills enable you to **analyse**, **interpret**, **process** and **evaluate** any information you have collected or acquired. These skills include:

✔ **Analytical Skills**

✔ **Counting Skills**

✔ **Design Skills (Poster/Bar Chart/Pie Chart/Diagram)**

✔ **Evaluation Skills**

✔ **Information-Processing Skills**

✔ **Publishing Skills**

✔ **Presentation Skills**

3. Communication Skills

These skills enable you to **communicate** and **engage** with other people, to participate in meaningful discussion and to present information or findings. These skills include:

✔ **Acting/Drama Skills**

✔ **Briefing Skills**

✔ **Chairing Meetings**

✔ **Compromising**

✔ **Defending a Viewpoint**

✔ **Delegation Skills**

✔ **Discussion Skills**

✔ **Listening Skills**

✔ **Negotiating Skills**

✔ **Organisational Skills**

✔ **Public Speaking Skills**

✔ **Reflection Skills**

4. Action Skills

These are practical skills which enable you to carry out your action project effectively. Examples of action skills include:

✔ **Budgeting Skills**

✔ **Campaigning Skills**

✔ **Decision-Making Skills**

✔ **Financial/Accounting Skills**

✔ **Fundraising Skills**

✔ **Hosting Skills**

✔ **Organisational Skills**

✔ **Publicity Skills**

✔ **Leadership Skills**

✔ **Planning Skills**

✔ **Typing Skills**

✔ **Problem-Solving Skills**

✔ **Voting Skills**

It is important to know the name of the skills you have used and how you applied those skills during the course of your action project.

Sample Report on an Action Project

A Fairtrade Awareness Day in my School

We were learning about Fairtrade in class and we all agreed that buying Fairtrade products was a good thing because it ensured that farmers in developing countries got a fair price for their produce. However, we were all surprised how little we knew about the Fairtrade products on sale in our local supermarkets. We all felt that it would be a good idea to raise awareness about Fairtrade and Fairtrade products in our school. But how to do it? We all shared our ideas and we finally agreed that the best way to raise awareness was to let some students and teachers in our school sample Fairtrade products.

Now we had to plan our action. We divided ourselves into committees and each committee had a particular job to do. The **permission committee** had to write a letter to our principal asking if we could hold our Fairtrade Awareness Day. The **contact committee** got in contact with Fairtrade Mark Ireland requesting posters and information. The **room committee** had to ask the home economics teacher for permission to use her classroom. They also had to organise the room for our Awareness Day.

Choose products with the Fairtrade Mark www.fairtrade.ie

Now we had to decide what Fairtrade products we would sample and where we would get them. The **research committee** searched on the Internet for a list of Fairtrade products available in Irish supermarkets. They also visited our local supermarkets and found out that some of the Fairtrade products on sale there included orange juice, tea, coffee, ice cream, chocolate, bananas, honey and chocolate sauce. The **produce committee** wrote a letter to the management of the supermarkets asking if they would donate some products for our Fairtrade Awareness Day. Thankfully our local supermarkets kindly donated all the products we wanted. The **invitation committee** designed and printed out invitations to our Fairtrade Awareness Day inviting both teachers and pupils to sample some products.

At last the day arrived. The **welcome committee** welcomed both teachers and students into the room and gave each person a small brochure on Fairtrade (supplied to us by Fairtrade Mark Ireland www.fairtrade.ie).

Each member of the **hosting committee** was responsible for one Fairtrade product. For example, the person in charge of Fairtrade tea had to organise the kettle, milk, sugar, cups and spoons. They also had to know what country the tea came from so they could inform our guests.

More than 60 people attended our Fairtrade Awareness Day. By far the most popular product was the Fairtrade ice cream accompanied by warm Fairtrade chocolate sauce!!

Overall we thought our action was a great success. Some of the guests who sampled the Fairtrade produce now buy these products on a weekly basis. I think our class has made a difference.

Student Task

1 What do the letters CSPE stand for?
2 What are the seven key concepts of CSPE?
3 Match the newspaper headlines on page 1 with their corresponding concepts (each headline links into more than one concept).
4 Name the four units of study in CSPE.
5 What is an active citizen? Can you think of any other famous active citizens besides the ones photographed on page 3?
6 What is an action project? Give five examples.

Rights and Responsibilities

In this section you will learn that every person is entitled to certain rights and to the protection of these rights. These rights enable each one of us to have our needs met and to live our lives with dignity. You will also realise that with rights come responsibilities. We have responsibilities towards other members of society, to the communities we belong to and to the environments we live in. Rights and responsibilities go hand in hand.

We will be focussing on:
- The individual's rights and responsibilities
- Rights and responsibilities in the community
- Ireland: the citizen's rights and responsibilities
- Rights and responsibilities: an international view.

The Individual's Rights and Responsibilities

Human needs

In order to survive and live life to the fullest, there are certain things that all humans need. Our most basic needs are food, clean water and shelter. Without these we cannot survive. We also have emotional needs – the need to feel safe and secure, and the need to be loved. Only when these needs are met can we fully develop as human beings. To illustrate this Abraham Maslow, an American psychologist, developed a hierarchy of human needs. Maslow believed that some needs were more important than others. Maslow uses a pyramid to represent this hierarchy. The bottom of the pyramid represents our most basic of needs. Only when these needs are met can we progress to level two of the pyramid. When level two needs are met then we can progress to the next level of the pyramid, and so on.

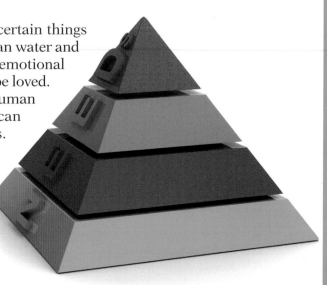

The need to develop fully as a human being — 5

Esteem needs – self-esteem, respect and recognition — 4

Love and belonging needs — 3

Safety, security and protection needs — 2

Survival needs – food, water, shelter, air, warmth — 1

Maslow's hierarchy of human needs

Wants

Wants are things that we would like or desire. Unlike needs, they are **not** vital to our survival or development. We need clothes, but we may want to be clothed in the latest designer brands. We do not, however, need designer clothes to survive. Designer clothes, therefore, are a want and not a need.

Student Task

1 What is meant by the term 'human needs'?
2 Distinguish between a want and a need.
3 Study the diagram here and decide which items are needs and which items are wants. When you have made your decision, write that item into the needs or wants column below.

Needs	Wants
1 _____	1 _____
2 _____	2 _____
3 _____	3 _____
4 _____	4 _____
5 _____	5 _____
6 _____	6 _____

Human Rights

By virtue of being human, every individual is entitled to certain rights and to the **protection** of these rights. Rights are essentially freedoms that enable every individual to have their needs met and develop fully as human beings. Everybody is entitled to these rights regardless of **race**, **nationality**, **age**, **gender**, **religion** and **social background**.

Social Rights   Economic Rights   Cultural Rights   Religious Rights   Civil Rights   Political Rights

A Brief History of Human Rights

A concern for human rights can be traced back thousands of years. Look at the Human Rights Timeline below to find out how human rights have developed throughout history.

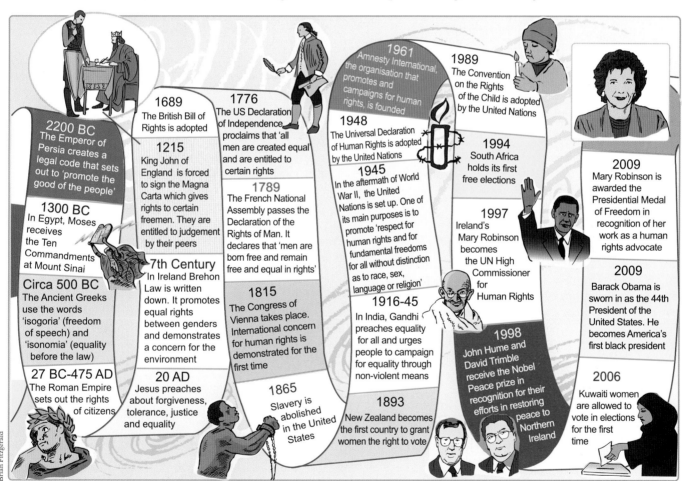

2200 BC The Emperor of Persia creates a legal code that sets out to 'promote the good of the people'

1300 BC In Egypt, Moses receives the Ten Commandments at Mount Sinai

Circa 500 BC The Ancient Greeks use the words 'isogoria' (freedom of speech) and 'isonomia' (equality before the law)

27 BC-475 AD The Roman Empire sets out the rights of citizens

20 AD Jesus preaches about forgiveness, tolerance, justice and equality

1689 The British Bill of Rights is adopted

1215 King John of England is forced to sign the Magna Carta which gives rights to certain freemen. They are entitled to judgement by their peers

7th Century In Ireland Brehon Law is written down. It promotes equal rights between genders and demonstrates a concern for the environment

1776 The US Declaration of Independence proclaims that 'all men are created equal' and are entitled to certain rights

1789 The French National Assembly passes the Declaration of the Rights of Man. It declares that 'men are born free and remain free and equal in rights'

1815 The Congress of Vienna takes place. International concern for human rights is demonstrated for the first time

1865 Slavery is abolished in the United States

1961 Amnesty International, the organisation that promotes and campaigns for human rights, is founded

1948 The Universal Declaration of Human Rights is adopted by the United Nations

1945 In the aftermath of World War II, the United Nations is set up. One of its main purposes is to promote 'respect for human rights and for fundamental freedoms for all without distinction as to race, sex, language or religion'

1916-45 In India, Gandhi preaches equality for all and urges people to campaign for equality through non-violent means

1893 New Zealand becomes the first country to grant women the right to vote

1989 The Convention on the Rights of the Child is adopted by the United Nations

1994 South Africa holds its first free elections

1997 Ireland's Mary Robinson becomes the UN High Commissioner for Human Rights

1998 John Hume and David Trimble receive the Nobel Peace prize in recognition for their efforts in restoring peace to Northern Ireland

2009 Mary Robinson is awarded the Presidential Medal of Freedom in recognition of her work as a human rights advocate

2009 Barack Obama is sworn in as the 44th President of the United States. He becomes America's first black president

2006 Kuwaiti women are allowed to vote in elections for the first time

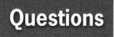
Brian Fitzgerald

As you can see, human rights have been important throughout history and throughout the world. Human rights remain very important in modern times.

Questions	Study the timeline above and answer the questions that follow:
	1 What civilisation was responsible for writing the first legal code?
	2 What was the Magna Carta?
	3 In what year was slavery abolished in the USA?
	4 In what year was the United Nations created?
	5 Who won the Nobel Peace Prize in 1998?

The Universal Declaration of Human Rights (UDHR)

In 1948, three years after the end of World War II, the **United Nations** issued **The Universal Declaration of Human Rights**. This declaration set out the rights that every person is entitled to. The UDHR contains 30 articles that outline the rights of all. Some of the most important rights contained in this declaration are outlined below.

Eleanor Roosevelt was a driving force behind the UDHR

What is a declaration?
A declaration is a formal statement. However, it is not legally binding.

- ✓ Everyone is born free and equal
- ✓ Everyone has the right not to be discriminated against
- ✓ Everyone has the right to life, liberty and freedom
- ✓ Everyone should be free from slavery
- ✓ Everyone has the right not to be tortured
- ✓ Everybody is equal before the law
- ✓ Everyone has the right to a fair trial
- ✓ Everyone has the right to be presumed innocent until proven guilty
- ✓ Every person has the right to privacy
- ✓ Everybody has the right to travel freely between countries
- ✓ Everyone has the right to asylum
- ✓ Everyone is entitled to a nationality
- ✓ Everyone has the right to marry
- ✓ Every person has the right to own property
- ✓ Everyone is entitled to freedom of thought, conscience and religion
- ✓ Everyone has the right to freedom of opinion and expression
- ✓ Everyone has the right to freedom of assembly
- ✓ Everyone has the right to vote and take part in government
- ✓ Everyone has the right to social security
- ✓ Everyone has the right to work and join a trade union
- ✓ Everybody has the right to rest and leisure
- ✓ Everybody has the right to an adequate standard of living
- ✓ Everyone has the right to an education

A date to remember!
International Human Rights Day – 10th December

Questions

1 Look at the photographs below. What right is represented by each photograph?

Photograph A

The right to _____?

Photograph B

The right to _____?

Photograph C

The right to _____?

Photograph D

The right to _____?

Photograph E

The right to _____?

Photograph F

The right to _____?

Student Task

1 Look back at the list of rights outlined in the UDHR. Write down the five rights you feel are the most important. Give reasons why you chose those particular rights.

2 Create a ' human rights wall' in your classroom to construct a visual representation of the UDHR. Each student is assigned one right and must come up with a picture or image that represents it. Pictures can be found in newspapers or magazines or drawn by you. When all the pictures have been collected, hang them on your 'human rights wall'.

The UN Convention on the Rights of the Child

Children are some of the most vulnerable members of society. Children all over the world are denied basic human rights so there is a real need to safeguard and protect their rights. With this in mind, the UN adopted the **Convention on the Rights of the Child** in **1989**. This sets down the rights to which **every** child is entitled. According to the Convention, **a child is any person under the age of 18**.

A convention is different from a declaration in that it **is** legally binding. Ireland **signed** the convention in 1990 and **ratified** it in 1992. (To ratify a convention means that a government makes a promise or a commitment to protect the rights laid down in that convention.)

The Convention on the Rights of the Child consists of 54 articles which can be broadly divided into four categories of rights:

1. Survival rights

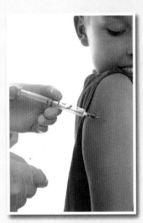

Every child is entitled to the most basic of rights – rights necessary for their survival. These include food, shelter, clean water, medical services and an adequate standard of living.

2. Development rights

Every child is entitled to develop fully as a human being. To develop fully, children need to be educated and they need to play and engage in leisure and cultural activities. Children also have the right of access to information.

3. Participation rights

Every child is entitled to become actively involved in their community and the nation they live in. Participation rights ensure that children can express their opinion on matters that affect them and also ensure that children are free to join associations.

4. Protection rights

These rights are very important as they safeguard the child from all forms of abuse, torture, cruelty, neglect and exploitation.

CONVENTION ON THE RIGHTS OF THE CHILD

Every child has:

the right to life;

the right to a name and nationality;

the right to be with their parents or with those who will care for them best;

the right to have a say about things that affect them;

the right to have ideas and say what they think;

the right to practice their religion;

the right to meet with other children;

the right to get information they need;

the right to special care, education and training, if needed;

the right to health care;

the right to enough food and clean water;

the right to free education;

the right to play;

the right to speak their own language;

the right to learn about and enjoy their own culture;

the right not to be used as a cheap worker;

the right not to be hurt or neglected;

the right not to be used as a soldier in wars;

the right to be protected from danger;

the right to know about their rights and responsibilities.

Know your rights.
Respect other people's rights.
Be responsible!

AMNESTY INTERNATIONAL — Irish Aid Department of Foreign Affairs An Roinn Gnóthaí Eachtracha — into Irish National Teachers' Organisation Cumann Múinteoirí Éireann — Foras na Gaeilge

Cross Border Primary Human Rights Education Initiative. Phone: Dublin 01- 863 8300 • Belfast 028 90 643000

Summary of Extract from the Convention on the Rights of the Child, adopted by the United Nations General Assembly, 20 November 1989.

Student Task

Study the poster above and answer the questions that follow:

1. Why, do you think, is it important to know your rights?
2. Find one article in the Convention that relates to each of the following;
   a. Survival rights
   b. Development rights
   c. Participation rights
   d. Protection rights
3. Choose three rights from the list above which you believe are the most important. Give a reason for each of your choices.

Read Sanjay's story and answer the questions that follow.
Sanjay's Story

My name is Sanjay. I am 12 years old and live in Calcutta, India. I live in a shanty town (a bustee) with my parents, my grandmother, my two brothers and my three sisters. Our home is very basic. It is made from planks of wood covered by tarpaulin (like a tent). With nine people living under the one roof, our conditions are very cramped. We have no flushing toilet or running water.

As you can see, my family is very poor. My father cannot find work but my mother works in a sewing factory for ten hours a day. Despite the long hours she gets paid very little. As a result my younger brother and I must work, so that there is enough food to feed my family.

For the past year I have been working in a carpet factory.

The factory owner employs mainly children because he does not have to pay us as much as adults. I begin work at 7.00am and finish at 6.30pm. I get just a 20 minute break a day. The factory owner supervises the workers every day. If he feels we are not working hard enough, or if we make a mistake, he often beats us or refuses to let us have a break.

I feel this is unfair, but I will not speak up in case I lose my job. When I got the job in the carpet factory I had to leave school. I can barely read or write. I wish I could go back to school.

Questions

1 What is a shanty town? Ask your geography teacher if you are unsure.
2 What basic needs does Sanjay and his family have?
3 Do you think that Sanjay is happy? Why?
4 Look at the Convention on the Rights of the Child and the UDHR. Make a list of rights that Sanjay and his family are being denied.
5 Compare Sanjay's life to yours. List some rights that you have under the UDHR which Sanjay does not have.

Rights in Conflict

Sometimes your rights may clash with the rights of others. This may cause conflict. Look at the cartoons below which highlight the ways in which the rights of one individual may conflict with the rights of another.

When our rights are in conflict with the rights of others, both parties need to reach a **compromise**. This means that each party must make allowances in some way for the rights of the other. Look at the cartoons below which outline the compromises made in each of the examples given above.

Questions

1 Have your rights ever been in conflict with the rights of others?
Write a paragraph outlining your experience.
2 Can you think of other examples of rights in conflict?
3 Can you think of a time when you made a compromise with someone?
Write a paragraph explaining how you reached that compromise.

Responsibilities

As well as rights we also have responsibilities towards other people, our communities, our country and the environment. Responsibilities go hand in hand with rights. If we neglect our responsibilities, the rights of others may be denied. Look at the examples on the next page which illustrate the ways in which rights and responsibilities go together.

It is important that we are aware of our responsibilities as well as our rights. Read the poem opposite which touches on the consequences of people not taking responsibility for others. It was written by Pastor Martin Niemöller.

Pastor Martin Niemöller was a Lutheran clergyman during Nazi Germany. In this poem he describes how, when the Nazis attacked different groups in German society, he did nothing. It is only when the Nazis attacked his own church that he decided to speak out.

It was, however, too late as there was no one left to speak out for him or his fellow clergymen.

First they came for the communists
And I didn't speak out -
Because I wasn't a communist.

Then they came for the Jews
And I didn't speak out
Because I wasn't a Jew.

Then they came for the trade unionists
And I didn't speak out -
Because I wasn't a trade unionist .

Then they came for the Catholics
And I didn't speak out -
Because I wasn't a Catholic.

Then they came for me -
And by that time no one was left
To speak out for me.

Questions

A. Read the poem by Pastor Niemöller and answer the questions that follow.

1 Why, do you think, was Pastor Niemöller unconcerned when the Nazis came for communists, Jews, trade-unionists and Catholics?
2 The poet tells us that he didn't speak up or defend these people.
  In your opinion, why was that?
3 Why was there no-one left to speak for him when he was arrested by the Nazis?
4 Describe the central message of this poem in your own words.

B. Match the right with the corresponding responsibility below.

Right	Responsibility
1 I have a right to have a picnic in the countryside	A while having the responsibility to respect the privacy of other people.
2 I have a right to take photographs	B while having the responsibility to turn up at the polling station on election day.
3 I have a right to say what I like about other people	C while having the responsibility to keep the countryside litter-free.
4 I have a right to build a nuclear plant	D while having the responsibility to respect the feelings of other people.
5 I have a right to vote	E while having the responsibility to protect the environment and the health and safety of others.

Animals Have Rights Too!

Animals, like humans, are entitled to live peaceful lives, free from torture, cruelty and neglect. Unlike humans, however, animals do not have a voice and they rely on us for protection. We all have a responsibility to protect the rights of animals who share the earth with us.

The following practices deny animals their rights:

- The fur trade
- Medical experiments on animals
- Cosmetic testing on animals
- Cruel agricultural practices
- Bloodsports
- Hunting.

Unfortunately there are daily reports of cruelty to animals in our newspapers. Here is one such story.

Nine Dogs Rescued from Appalling Conditions

A confidential complaint from a member of the public to the National Cruelty Helpline, resulted in nine dogs being removed from a premises in the Ballinalee area of Longford. The area and condition that the animals were in were described as 'appalling' by ISPCA staff.

The areas in which the dogs had been restricted were described as very dirty and soiled, with no provisions for bedding and no evidence of access to food or water. Upon further examination of the property, the bodies of three dead puppies were found huddled in a corner of the filthy shed. The nine dogs that were rescued from the property all suffered extreme levels of neglect. The neglect ranged from many ailments, severe emaciation, open wounds, infestation of worms and fleas, mange, tartar, canker, all dogs exhibited a degree of trauma (listlessness) and suffered with filthy or matted coats.

The veterinary surgeon stated: 'It is clear from my examination that the dogs have been neglected, malnourished, kept in filthy conditions and denied basic veterinary treatment over a prolonged period of time'.

Source: www.ispca.ie, August 2009

Questions

1 What helpline did the member of the public ring?
2 Describe the conditions the dogs were living in.
3 What rights were the dogs in this article denied?
4 Do you think that the dogs' owner deserves to be punished? Give a reason for your answer.

The Zoo Debate

Almost all of us have visited a zoo at some point in our lives. However, there is much debate as to whether zoos deprive animals of their rights. Those who believe zoos are important argue that:

- Zoos promote an appreciation of the animal world
- Zoos educate the public about animals not native to their country
- Zoos play an important role in the conservation of endangered species
- Zoos are instrumental in animal research.

Those who are against zoos argue that:

- Animals do not live in their natural habitats
- Animals are forced to spend their entire lives in enclosures that are often too small for them
- Animals are sometimes unable to engage in natural behaviour, such as flying, hunting, running, climbing, scavenging or choosing mating partners
- Animals can lack mental stimulation that can lead them to behaving abnormally. Abnormal and self-destructive behaviour, called 'zoochosis', can result. Signs of zoochosis include repeated head-bobbing, biting cage bars and even self-mutilation.

YOUR CALL!

DO YOU THINK ZOOS PROTECT OR DENY ANIMAL RIGHTS? Write a speech to defend your viewpoint.

Protecting Animal Rights – The ISPCA

The ISPCA (Irish Society for the Prevention of Cruelty to Animals) was set up to prevent animal cruelty and to promote the welfare of animals in Ireland. The ISPCA believes that humans have a responsibility for the welfare of the animals with whom we share the planet. The ISPCA has many branches throughout the country and its work includes:

- Animal rescue and rehabilitation
- Re-homing animals that have been neglected, abused or lost
- Providing advice on the care of pets and other animals.

Animal Welfare

Animal welfare involves looking after domestic pets and caring for them so that they can live healthy lives. It also involves making sure that farm animals that are bred for food, such as cows, pigs and sheep, do not suffer unnecessarily during long-distance transportation or during the slaughtering process.

Most of us have owned a pet at some time in our lives. It is important that we care for them properly. Can you think of some responsibilities that a dog-owner has? Fill them out in the spaces below.

The ISPCA has even issued a declaration on the rights of animals.

Declaration on the Rights of Animals

That we share the earth with other creatures great and small

That many of these animals experience pleasure and pain

That these animals deserve our just treatment and that these animals are unable to speak for themselves.

We do therefore declare that these animals:

- Have the right to live free from wanton exploitation whether in the name of science or sport, exhibition or service, food or fashion

- Have the right to live in harmony with their nature, rather than according to human desires

- Have the right to live on a healthy planet.

We therefore call for the protection of these rights.

(www.ispca.ie)

Responsibilities of a Dog Owner

1 _____

2 _____

3 _____

4 _____

5 _____

Questions

Study the poster above and answer the questions that follow:
1 What organisation is responsible for this poster?
2 What is the central message of this poster?
3 Why do you think the organisation responsible for this poster used a famous person to promote its message?
4 Briefly describe one action your class could undertake to make students in your school more aware of the fur trade and its impact on animals.

There are many other organisations that promote animal welfare and campaign for animal rights in Ireland.

Irish organisations include:

Compassion in
World Farming

Irish Council Against
Blood Sports

Irish Seal Sanctuary

Sathya Sai Sanctuary
Trust for Nature

25

Wordsearch on the Individual's Rights and Responsibilities
Complete the following wordsearch

D	Z	P	T	X	R	Q	W	M	V	M	U	R	V	B	P	Z	R	C	S
U	E	Q	C	F	I	I	D	V	C	P	U	S	D	P	M	Q	P	E	R
B	Q	C	I	V	W	H	G	Z	D	F	U	H	Z	I	J	R	I	S	K
K	O	G	L	N	Z	I	R	H	N	O	B	G	U	B	A	T	X	B	I
O	H	O	F	A	I	U	N	I	T	E	D	N	A	T	I	O	N	S	C
O	P	Z	N	C	R	E	H	S	R	S	F	T	I	L	B	X	W	T	O
M	S	O	O	R	R	A	L	G	Z	Q	I	F	I	Y	D	S	C	A	N
R	R	U	C	R	G	A	T	S	L	V	Y	B	J	Y	N	O	A	I	V
R	T	K	F	B	M	V	T	I	P	A	I	X	Q	P	M	S	Y	H	E
L	Q	T	L	I	R	I	Y	M	O	S	V	A	F	P	Q	H	W	C	N
G	E	L	N	Y	G	W	N	I	N	N	M	I	R	C	D	W	T	Z	T
U	A	A	E	G	Q	B	N	O	Z	E	J	O	V	E	L	Y	A	Q	I
W	E	L	F	A	R	E	P	H	V	I	M	H	V	R	B	D	G	X	O
E	M	Y	R	L	N	S	K	D	Y	I	N	B	J	O	U	X	P	G	N
C	A	S	D	E	E	N	L	A	S	R	E	V	I	N	U	S	I	S	W
J	S	F	A	R	E	A	V	E	P	M	H	P	Z	P	D	P	Q	Y	R
P	L	E	Z	U	X	L	X	C	V	G	T	Z	H	W	J	B	M	I	C
T	O	C	K	G	I	Q	M	G	U	X	W	U	N	Y	G	F	T	B	P
F	W	O	D	C	Z	Z	F	I	D	H	J	Y	I	U	S	I	Y	S	V
R	B	E	G	F	O	U	H	Q	R	E	F	E	S	U	L	D	V	I	H

■ ANIMALS   ■ DECLARATION   ■ RESPONSIBILITIES   ■ UNIVERSAL
■ COMPROMISE   ■ MASLOW   ■ RIGHTS   ■ WELFARE
■ CONFLICT   ■ NEEDS   ■ SURVIVAL
■ CONVENTION   ■ RATIFY   ■ UNITED NATIONS

2.1

IDEAS FOR TAKING ACTION:

→ Celebrate International Human Rights Day in your school (10th December). The celebration might include a poster display or a play focusing on a human rights issue.

→ Hold an animal rights awareness campaign in your school.

→ Invite a guest speaker from:
  – A human rights organisation
  – An animal rights organisation.

→ Organise a visit to:
  – A local ISPCA centre
  – An animal rescue centre.

→ Organise a fundraising activity for:
  – A human rights organisation
  – An animal rights organisation.

SKILLS YOU MIGHT USE:

→ Organisation   → Communication   → Research   → Financial
→ Drama   → Teamwork   → Public relations   → Letter-writing
→ Artistic   → Hosting   → Telephone   → Negotiation
→ Questioning

Can you think of other skills you may need to undertake these actions?

CHAPTER *2.2*

Rights and Responsibilities in the Community

What is a Community?

A community can be described as a **group of people** who have something in **common** with each other. Members of a community may share a common place, common goals or common interests. Throughout your life you will belong to many communities. Examples of communities include:

→ **Your family**

→ **Your youth club**

→ **Your neighbourhood**

→ **Your sports team**

Student Task

Can you name three more examples of communities?

1 _____

2 _____

3 _____

New School — New Community

Schools are also communities. You have something in common with the people that belong to your school community.

School crest

Classmates

MY SCHOOL COMMUNITY

Teachers

School building

School uniform

School teams/clubs

Student Task

Let's see how well you know your school and the people who share that community with you. In the boxes below fill in the following:

1 A drawing/sketch of your school crest

2 A drawing/sketch of your school uniform

3 The names of five classmates

4 The name of your tutor/class teacher

5 The name of your Principal

6 The address of your school

School Rules

The school community is shared by many people – students, teachers, staff and parents. The common goal shared by these members is your education. For that goal to be achieved, it is important to have school rules. Rules are crucial because they ensure that:

■ Everyone is treated equally and fairly
■ Every student is given the opportunity to reach his or her full potential
■ The school community is a healthy and safe environment for all
■ The rights of everyone within the school community are respected and protected.

John's First Week in School

At last! My first week as a first-year student has come to an end. It hasn't been all bad, I suppose. I quite like my new school. A lot of my friends from primary school are in my class so I feel right at home. I also enjoy some of the subjects I have never studied before, like French, woodwork and technical graphics.

However, I find this school much stricter than my primary school. On Tuesday, I was given 100 lines for not having my homework done. On Wednesday, my tutor gave out to me because I was seen racing down the corridor with Conor Murray. On Thursday, I was caught chewing gum in Mr Ryan's class.

When I received a very long tongue-lashing from Mr Ryan, he explained to me that just the other day chewing gum got stuck on another student's uniform and the boy in question had to buy a new pair of trousers. I certainly wouldn't like that to happen to me! Now I'm beginning to understand why rules are important in my school.

Questions

1 What rules did John break in his first week in school?
2 Why, do you think, did John's tutor give out to him for running down the corridor?
3 When did John realise that school rules are important?
4 Look at your school rules. Pick out the five rules you feel are the most important. Explain why you chose those rules.
5 Do you think that students should be involved in drawing up school rules? Give reasons for your answers.
6 Give three reasons why school rules are important.

IMAGINE!

IMAGINE THERE WERE NO RULES IN YOUR SCHOOL
Write an account of what a typical day in your school would be like.

Rights and Responsibilities in the School Community

Every member of the school community – students, teachers, administrative staff and parents – are entitled to certain rights and to the protection of these rights. However, we also have responsibilities towards each other and the school community as a whole. One way in which your class can explore and think more about their rights and responsibilities is by drawing up a **class charter of rights and responsibilities**.

1 Get into pairs or small groups and come up with at least six rights that each student in your class is entitled to as a member of your school community
2 Each group will report back to the class and the teacher will write each idea on the blackboard
3 The class will vote on their favourite six rights
4 In pairs or small groups, now come up with a responsibility that corresponds or relates to your chosen rights.
5 To help you on your way, one right and its corresponding responsibility have been included in the charter overleaf. Nominate two students from your class to copy the class charter on to a large sheet of paper and hang it on the classroom wall.

Our Class Charter of Rights and Responsibilities

We have a right to an education
We have a responsibility to do our best in class

We have a right _____
We have a responsibility _____

We have a right _____
We have a responsibility _____

We have a right _____
We have a responsibility _____

We have a right _____
We have a responsibility _____

We have a right _____
We have a responsibility _____

We have a right _____
We have a responsibility _____

Ideas For Taking Action 2.2

→ Design a booklet for incoming first-year students. The booklet might contain a map of your school, a list of teachers and subjects, a list of the various school clubs and a copy of the school rules.

SKILLS YOU MIGHT USE:
→ Teamwork
→ Computer
→ Discussion
→ Interviewing
→ Research
→ Information gathering
→ Publishing

Can you think of other skills you may need to undertake this action?

Ireland: The Citizen's Rights and Responsibilities

Being an Irish citizen entitles you to certain rights, and also to the protection of these rights. These rights include:

→ **The right to hold an Irish passport**

→ **The right to own property**

→ **The right to vote in elections**

→ **The right to marry.**

Can you think of three other rights Irish citizens are entitled to?

Citizen Information Centres

Citizen Information Centres (CICs) are located throughout Ireland and provide Irish citizens with information and advice on a wide range of issues. By contacting or visiting one of these centres, Irish citizens can find out about their rights and entitlements.

Questions | Study the website page above and answer these questions.

1 Where is the Citizens Information Centre featured on this webpage?
2 Describe the service it offers to citizens?
3 This CIS gives information and advice on a range of topics. List five of them.
4 How many citizens per year avail of these services?
5 List three forms provided by Tallaght Citizens Information Centre.
6 What are this centre's opening hours?

Responsibilities and the Citizen

By now you are aware that responsibilities go hand in hand with rights. Being a responsible citizen means that you must respect the rights of other citizens and act in a responsible way.

As an Irish citizen, one of your basic rights is to own property, for example a car. However, owning a car comes with responsibilities. These include the responsibility to:

Possess a valid driving licence

Have adequate insurance

Observe speed limits

Obey traffic laws

Drive carefully

Use fuels that are environmentally friendly

Respect the rights of other drivers and pedestrians

FIND OUT!

Find out more about the rights and entitlements of Irish citizens. Check out the website www.citizensinformation.ie

Study the citizen profiles below, and in your exercise book fill in the responsibilities of each citizen:

A. Citizen Jane – Jane is 18 years old. She has just received her polling card in the post as she is now eligible to vote in forthcoming local elections.

Jane has a responsibility to .... ?

B. Citizen Paul – Paul owns the local pub. His pub is situated right next door to a housing estate. On Friday and Saturday nights a DJ plays in the pub. Some of the residents feel that the music is too loud.

Paul has a responsibility to .... ?

C. Citizen Jim – Jim owns the local chip shop. The outside of his shop is often strewn with empty chip-bags and bottles. The residents of his town have plans to enter the Tidy Towns Competition.

Jim has a responsibility to .... ?

D. Citizen Anne – Anne has lived in her house for the past year. Every week she leaves out her bins for collection. She recently received notification from her local authority that her bin tax is due.

Anne has a responsibility to ....?

E. Citizen Rose – Rose works in the local newsagent. A group of boys aged about 12 have come into the shop and have asked to buy cigarettes.

Rose has a responsibility to ....?

Protecting Human Rights – The Work of Irish Citizens

There are many Irish citizens who work tirelessly for the rights of others and have made a huge impact on the lives they have touched.

Fr Peter McVerry

Peter McVerry has been working with Dublin's young homeless for the past 30 years. He has campaigned for the rights of these young people during this time. He began his ministry in Dublin's inner city in 1974 and found that many young men were living on the streets. Some had left abusive homes whilst others were homeless due to drug or alcohol addiction. In response to this he opened a hostel for the young homeless to stay in. In 1983 he set up the Arrupe Society, a charity that provided accommodation and support for the young homeless. This charity was renamed the **Peter McVerry Trust** in 2005. This trust provides a wide range of services to the young homeless including an outreach service, emergency accommodation, de-tox programmes, drug-free aftercare accomodation and supported housing.

Christina Noble

Born into poverty in Dublin in the 1940s, Christina Noble had a dream to help children who, like herself, were deprived of their basic needs and rights. Her dream brought her to Vietnam in 1989 where thousands of children live in extreme poverty. Christina soon set up the **Christina Noble Children's Foundation**, a voluntary organisation that aims to provide nutrition, medical care and education for poor children in Vietnam and their families. The foundation is also instrumental in the protection of children at risk from all forms of exploitation. Recently Christina Noble expanded the work of her foundation into Mongolia.

Niall Mellon

On a visit to Cape Town in South Africa in 2002, Niall Mellon visited some of the townships where the poorest families lived. He was appalled by the conditions they were living in. He decided to set up the **Niall Mellon Township Trust** the same year in order to provide quality housing in the most impoverished areas. Every year this trust organises a week-long 'building blitz' where skilled volunteers travel to South Africa to offer their services and build houses for various communities. To date, thousands of houses have been built in various townships in South Africa.

Adi Roche

In 1986 the world experienced the worst human-made disaster in history – the explosion of the Chernobyl nuclear power plant in Ukraine, Russia. Many people lost their lives and of those that survived, many soon developed serious illnesses and diseases as a result of the high levels of radiation that occurred. In the aftermath thousands of children were born with disabilities, deformities and serious illnesses. Many were placed in orphanages because their parents could not provide them with the care they needed. Cork woman Adi Roche recognised the plight of these children and in 1991 she founded the **Chernobyl Children's Project**. The project sent convoys of trucks with much-needed humanitarian aid and medical supplies to affected communities. The project has also brought children with serious illness and disabilities to Europe, where they have undergone life-saving and life-changing operations.

Other people who have worked for the protection of human rights in Ireland include:

→ **Willie Bermingham**

→ **John Hume**

→ **Mary Robinson**

→ **Sister Stanislaus Kennedy**

Can you name some others?

FACT!
The Minister for Justice, Equality and Law Reform is responsible for the protection of human rights in Ireland.

WALKING DEBATE!
Irish citizens are responsible citizens.

IMAGINE!
You are a high profile sports person. Write a paragraph describing how you could use your celebrity to influence politicians and work for the rights of others.

Ideas For Taking Action 2.3

→ Invite a guest speaker from:
  – your local Citizen Information Centre   – the Chernobyl Children's Project
  – the Niall Mellon Township Trust   – the Christina Noble Children's Foundation.
  – the Peter McVerry Trust

→ Organise a fundraising activity for a human rights organisation. The activity could be a:
  – cake sale   – non-uniform day   – table quiz
  – raffle   – sponsored walk or marathon.

SKILLS YOU MIGHT USE:

→ Baking	→ Research	→ Financial	→ Organisational
→ Computer	→ Public relations	→ Letter-writing	→ Telephone
→ Hosting	→ Questioning.		

Can you think of other skills you may need to undertake your actions?

Rights and Responsibilities: An International View

Amnesty International

Amnesty International is a worldwide organisation which works and campaigns for human rights, particularly in countries where there is a history of human rights abuses. Set up in 1961 by Peter Beneson, a British lawyer, Amnesty International's vision is:

'*...of a world in which every person enjoys all the human rights enshrined in the Universal Declaration of Human Rights and other international human rights standards.*'

Amnesty International is the largest human rights organisation in the world with a membership of 150 million people. It encourages its members to put pressure on governments to end human rights abuses. In addition, this organisation also co-ordinates letter-writing campaigns, petitions, fundraising drives and public demonstrations to increase worldwide awareness of human rights issues.

The main aims of Amnesty International are:
1 To promote an awareness of human rights issues.

2 To campaign for an end to human rights abuses such as:
   – The death penalty
   – Violence against women
   – Prisoners of conscience – individuals who have been imprisoned because of their political, religious or other beliefs
   – Child labour
   – The inhumane treatment of prisoners
   – All forms of cruelty and torture
   – Child soldiers
   – Worker exploitation
   – Racism
   – Abuses against refugees.

Questions

1 Who founded Amnesty International and in what year?
2 How many members belong to Amnesty International?
3 What are the main aims of Amnesty International?
4 What tools are used to promote awareness of human rights abuses worldwide?
5 Name five other organisations that work and campaign for human rights?

Nelson Mandela – Human Rights Activist

There are many people in the world who have devoted much of their lives to the protection of human rights. Nelson Mandela is one such person. He was born in South Africa in 1918. At that time South Africa was ruled by a white minority (less than 20% of the population was white). In 1948 the government introduced the policy of **apartheid**. This means 'separateness' in the Afrikaans language. This policy had severe consequences for the native black population.

By law black South Africans could not:
→ Choose where they lived – they had to live in black townships
→ Have certain jobs
→ Vote in elections
→ Attend certain schools and colleges
→ Marry a white person
→ Mix freely with white people. Separate facilities for black and white people were created. A black person had to use a 'black' toilet or sit in the 'black' section of a restaurant.

Mandela became a lawyer and joined the **African National Congress** (**ANC**), a peaceful civil rights organisation that promoted the interests of the black African population. Apartheid resulted in strict racial

ALAMY

divisions in South Africa and denied the black population their basic human rights. Mandela spoke out against the discrimination his people were subjected to. In 1960 the white government outlawed the ANC. As a result it operated as an underground organisation and formed a military wing. In 1964 Mandela was arrested and put into prison for his membership of the ANC. He stayed in prison for 27 years until the ANC was legalised under a new South African government led by F. W. de Klerk. De Klerk also ended apartheid in 1991. Mandela was then released from prison.

Since his release Mandela has worked ceaselessly for human rights. He has spoken up against those who oppress, discriminate, abuse or exploit. In 1993, Nelson Mandela and F. W. de Klerk were awarded the Nobel Peace Prize for their efforts to bring about equality in South Africa. In 1994, Nelson Mandela became the President of South Africa, a position he held until 1999. He is still an active advocate for many social and human rights organisations.

Nelson Mandela took responsibility for the rights of others. For many he has been a symbol of hope, especially for the millions of people worldwide who are denied their rights on a daily basis.

Questions

1 What was apartheid?
2 What rights were the black South Africans denied under apartheid?
3 Why was Mandela imprisoned?
4 How long did Mandela remain in prison?
5 Why is Mandela a symbol of hope to so many people?

FIND OUT!

Find out more about an international organisation that campaigns for human rights.

Crossword on Rights and Responsibilities

Across
4 He developed a hierarchy of human needs.
5 These information centres provide free information.
6 An organisation promoting animal welfare in Ireland.
7 Every individual is entitled to these.
8 This policy led to racial divisions in South Africa.
9 It is important that we obey these in our school community

Down
1 This international organisation protects human rights worldwide: _____ International
2 These go hand in hand with rights.
3 This Christina helps poor families in Vietnam.
4 The surname of a famous South African human rights activist.

Word bank

- → RULES
- → AMNESTY
- → RIGHTS
- → NOBLE
- → APARTHEID
- → MANDELA
- → CITIZEN
- → ISPCA
- → RESPONSIBILITIES
- → MASLOW

Ideas For Taking Action

2.4

→ Invite a guest speaker from:
  - Amnesty International
  - Concern
  - Trócaire
  - Oxfam
  - Any other human rights organisation.

→ Organise a fundraising event for a human rights organisation.

→ Organise a campaign about a human rights issue your class feels strongly about.

You could:
  - Circulate a petition
  - Start a letter-writing campaign
  - Lobby your local politicians.

SKILLS YOU MIGHT USE:

→ Surveying	→ Organisation	→ Hosting
→ Petition design	→ Public relations	→ Questioning
→ Telephone	→ Financial	→ Letter-writing.

Can you think of other skills you may need to undertake your action?

Rights and Responsibilities – Past Examination Questions

1 Complete the following sentence:

The Universal D_____ of H_____ R_____ was signed in 1948 in order to protect Human Rights around the world.

2 The following photographs are of four human rights activists. Using the space provided, match the name of each activist with the human rights activity they are involved in.

You may use each NAME and ACTIVITY only ONCE.

Aung San Suu Kyi   Nelson Mandela   Adi Roche   Bono

Protesting for civil rights in Burma   Campaigning against world debt
Caring for children in Chernobyl   Working for democracy in Africa

Name: _____

Activity: _____

Name: _____

Activity:_____

Name: _____

Activity:_____

Name:_____

Activity:_____

(CSPE paper, 2009)

3 Your CSPE class has decided to produce a booklet about the school for new First Years as an Action Project that would benefit the school community.
 (a) Name and describe **THREE** groups that **YOUR CLASS** would set up in order to undertake this Action Project.
 (b) Name **FOUR** different things that you would include in this booklet and explain why they would help new First Years coming into your school.
 (c) Name and explain **TWO** skills that you would use while producing this booklet.

(CSPE Paper, 2009)

4 Imagine you have been given the job of compiling a **Charter of Prisoners' Rights and Responsibilities**.
 (a) Name **THREE** organisations that you would contact to help make this Charter as meaningful as possible.
 (b) List **TWO** important rights and **TWO** important responsibilities you think should be included in the list.
 (c) In the case of **EACH** of these rights and responsibilities explain why you think this particular right or responsibility should be included.

(CSPE Paper, 2001)

Website Watch
Check out the following websites which will give you further information on some of the issues raised in this section.

Human rights	**Children's rights**	**Animal Rights**
www.amnesty.ie	www.unicef.ie	www.ispca.ie
www.trocaire.org	www.barnardos.ie	www.peta.org
www.hrw.org	www.childrensrights.ie	www.aran.ie
www.un.org	www.ispcc.ie	www.animalrights.net
www.ihrc.ie		

TAKING ACTION

A visit to an animal rescue centre or local ISPCA

A good way of finding out more about animal welfare and rights is to visit a local animal rescue centre or the ISPCA.

Worked Example

1 The Plan → 2 Committees → 3 The Visit → 4 Review

The plan:

What preparation do we, as a class, need to do?
How do we get to the animal centre?
When will we visit?
What do we need to find out?
Who can help us in our preparation?

Committees:

How many committees do we need?
What are the responsibilities of each committee?

PERMISSION COMMITTEE — CONTACT COMMITTEE — TRANSPORT COMMITTEE

THANK YOU COMMITTEE — FINANCE COMMITTEE — QUESTIONS COMMITTEE — ORGANISATION COMMITTEE

Can you think of any other committees you might need for this action?

The visit:

On the morning of the visit you should give whoever is transporting you to the centre a call just to confirm what time you are leaving at. It is also important to ensure that everyone in your class is aware of the time of visit and the meeting point.

Animal centres are very busy places so be aware of the ground rules you must observe during the visit. Perhaps the contact committee could ask the centre director what is or is not allowed during the course of the visit (for example, eating).

The review:

A review of the action is essential as it enables you to measure how successful the visit was. During the review there are a number of questions you can ask yourself:

Was the action a success? Why? Why not?
Would I do anything differently?
What did I learn?
What skills did I use?
Have my opinions changed as a result of the visit?

Skills You Might Use:

→ Letter writing
→ Telephone skills
→ Financial skills
→ Communication skills
→ Interview skills
→ Listening skills.

Human Dignity

In Section Two you learned that every human being has needs and is entitled to basic human rights to meet them. These rights enable people to live with dignity. Loss of human dignity occurs when basic human needs are not provided for, or when certain rights are being denied to an individual or to a group. This can lead to humiliation, degradation and isolation. The concept of **human dignity** is closely linked to the concept of **rights and responsibilities**.

Human Dignity and the Individual

What is Human Dignity?

Every human being is entitled to live his or her life with dignity. This can be achieved if individuals' basic needs are met and their rights are respected. However, if these basic needs – clean water, food and shelter, for example – are denied to an individual, then there is a loss of that person's human dignity. Such loss can also occur if an individual is denied basic human rights, such as the right to be treated equally. A loss of human dignity can have very serious consequences for the person involved. It can lead to isolation, deprivation, degradation and humiliation.

Protecting human dignity involves treating people equally and with respect, regardless of colour, religion, social background, race, sexual orientation, age or gender. There is a responsibility for all of us to respect the lifestyles of others.

Prejudice

Prejudice occurs when we prejudge an individual or group, usually negatively, without actually meeting or knowing that person or those people. There are many individuals or groups in society that are victims of prejudice. These include:

→ Refugees and asylum seekers

→ Persons with disabilities

→ Older persons

→ The Traveller community

→ Young people

→ Women

> **Can you think of any other groups of people who are victims of prejudice?**

Study the poster below and answer the questions that follow.

Which man is a gang member?

Questions

1 Which of these men is most likely to be in a gang, in your opinion?
2 Do you think that you are guilty of prejudice in making your decision? Give a reason for your answer.

One form of prejudice is **stereotyping**.

Stereotyping

Stereotyping occurs when we **label** an individual or group of people, usually in a negative way. For example, in Hollywood films the Irish are often portrayed as drunks or lovers of fist fights. This is a very narrow view of the Irish people and it labels them in a damaging way. Some Hollywood directors are, therefore, guilty of stereotyping or labelling Irish people.

As individuals we can often label or stereotype others because of their accents, the way they dress, the area they come from or the communities they belong to. Stereotyping can lead to a loss of human dignity. Read Peter's story:

Peter's Story

My name is Peter. I am a member of the Traveller community. I have lived in eight different places during my 12 years. I have recently moved to a site just outside Cork city and have just started a new school. On my first day in school a number of my new classmates asked me some questions about myself. I told them I was a member of the Traveller community. 'You must be joking!' said one girl. 'Sure all knackers are scruffy!' I didn't reply to this girl as her comment made me feel very bad, even though it was meant as a compliment. I was also very angry because some of the members of my community have sanitary facilities and wash every day, just like people in the settled community. I also hate being called a 'knacker' - it's a very disrespectful word. As you can see, my first day at school didn't go so smoothly, but since then things have got better. I have made many new friends in my class who like me for who I am, and not where I come from. I am doing well in class, am a member of the school soccer team and, last week, I was awarded Tidiest Boy in the Class!

Questions

1 In what way was Peter a victim of stereotyping?
2 How did Peter feel when the girl made comments about him?
3 Describe how Peter has proved the stereotype wrong?
4 Can you think of some other members of society who are stereotyped?

Discrimination

Discrimination occurs when individuals or groups are **treated unfairly** because of factors such as:

- Skin colour
- Age
- Race
- Disability.

- Religion
- Gender
- Social background

Discrimination can take many forms. Some of the most common forms include:

- Refusing access to services, such as pubs or hotels, because of skin colour or disability
- Failure to provide facilities or access for the disabled in public places or on public transport
- Failure to employ or promote an individual on the basis of gender, age, skin colour, disability, race, etc.

> **Questions**
> 1 What is discrimination?
> 2 List five factors that contribute to discrimination.
> 3 Name and describe one way in which an individual or group can be discriminated against.

Persons with Disabilities: a Human Dignity Issue

PHOTOCALL 2, CAMERAPRESS 3

Persons with disabilities, like everybody else, are entitled to be treated with respect and to live their lives with dignity. However, many people with disabilities experience forms of prejudice and discrimination on a daily basis. This stems from negative attitudes and a lack of understanding towards those with disabilities. Types of discrimination encountered include:

- Lack of job opportunities
- Lack of services
- Poor access for those with physical disabilities
- Lack of educational opportunities
- Negative attitudes towards disability.

There are approximately 500 million people throughout the world who have some form of disability. Many of these people feel that their needs are not being met and that they are not given the same chances as able-bodied people, resulting in a loss of human dignity. This is despite the fact that although disabled in some way, these people possess a wide variety of abilities and talents and make a huge contribution to society.

Disabled man gets €3k over egg attack by rail staff

A wheelchair user had an egg thrown at him by disgruntled rail staff, angry that he had to use the dining car when travelling on the train.

William Hennessy, who is in his 40s and now living in Dublin, was awarded €3,000 by the Equality Tribunal after it was found he had been harassed by staff attached to Network Catering on Irish Rail.

Mr Hennessy told the tribunal that a change in the regulations in 1999 meant he could no longer park his wheelchair in the baggage area of the train.

He had to park his wheelchair in a designated spot in the dining car, but as he needed a motorised wheelchair, which is larger than a manual wheelchair, space was tight and his wheelchair often jutted out into the aisle.

POSED BY MODELS, SHUTTERSTOCK

In addition to being refused access to the train on a number of occasions, Mr Hennessy said in the dining car he came to feel maligned by staff members who believed he was taking up space that might have been used by customers. He said the service trolley was rammed into his wheelchair as it moved past, and

staff would ask him to move, even though they knew he needed assistance.

On April 27, 2000, he exited the train at Kent Station in Cork and an egg was thrown at him from the direction of the dining car.

The Equality Tribunal said it was "an undisputed fact" that an egg was thrown after Mr Hennessy left the train on April 27, 2000,

and that he ultimately received a written apology.

Irish Rail was ordered to display a visible notice that "passengers with disabilities are welcome to travel and enjoy the amenity of the train without interference".

Mr Hennessy welcomed the tribunal's decision but said "the award will not even pay for one wheel-chair damaged on the train".

(Source: by Noel Baker, *Irish Examiner*, 16 June 2009)

Class Discussion

1 Why was Mr Hennessy awarded €3,000 at an equality tribunal?
2 Why, do you think, was Mr Hennessy refused access to trains on a number of occasions?
3 In what ways did Mr Hennessy suffer a loss of human dignity?
4 How, do you think, did Mr Hennessy feel when an egg was thrown at him?
5 Can you think of some ways in which trains can be made more accessible to persons with disabilities?

Support for Persons with Disabilities

Organisations that support persons with disabilities include:

- Disability Federation of Ireland
- Enable Ireland
- Irish Wheelchair Association
- National Council for the Blind in Ireland
- Paralympic Council of Ireland
- Special Olympics Ireland
- Rehab.

Date to remember! International Day of the Disabled – 3rd December

Questions

1. Choose one of the organisations above and briefly describe its work.
2. It has often been said that 'Attitudes are the real disability'. Do you agree with this statement? Why or why not?
3. What actions could your class or school take to raise awareness on the issue of disability? Briefly describe three possible actions.

Brainstorm

Three new students have joined your school:

Anne is blind.
David is deaf.
Julie can't walk and is a wheelchair user.

1. Think about your school building, your classrooms and the school day. Can you think of one problem that each of these new students may encounter in your school on a daily basis?
2. Now think of some ways these problems can be overcome so that each student's needs are met and their human dignity is respected.

Racism

Racism is based on the assumption that some races or ethnic groups are superior to others. According to the National Consultative Committee on Racism and Inter-culturalism (the NCCRI), racism is on the rise in Ireland.

Racism is a form of discrimination directed at members of minority ethnic groups. Victims of racism have reported that:

- People have made hurtful remarks about them
- They have been harassed and verbally abused on the street
- They have been refused access to goods and services
- They have been the victims of physical aggression and assault.

Racism deprives individuals of their human dignity. Adetoyse Kemi, formerly from Nigeria, is a pupil of the Kings Inns secondary school in Dublin. In the following interview, Adetoyse describes the abuse and harassment she endures because of the colour of her skin:

We are usually told to 'f... off back to where you came from' or they call us 'black monkeys,' she said. She told of taxi and bus drivers shutting bus doors and speeding off before she can board. Or how 'sometimes, when I sit down, the person beside me will get up and go elsewhere'.
'I don't understand it,' she said. 'Where I come from, if we saw whites we welcomed them warmly. But it's not just blacks. It applies to Russians or Chinese as well. People don't want us. Any of us.'

(Source: 'Intuition', *Irish Independent*, Volume 4, No. 7)

<table>
<tr><td>

Date to remember!

International Day Against Racism – 21st March

</td><td>

WALKING DEBATE

Irish people are not racist.

</td></tr>
</table>

Show Racism the Red Card!

Show Racism the Red Card is an organisation that uses high-profile footballers and sportspeople to educate young people about racism and its consequences. Many footballers in particular have been subjected to racist chants from supporters from opposing teams. They have joined the Red Card campaign to make people more aware of the effects of racism.

Let's see what some sports stars have to say about racism.

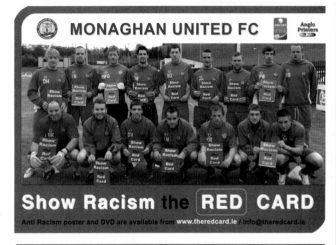

You have to look beyond race because as a human being you have to experience the person from the inside first.
Henrik Larsson, football star

People who have moved to Ireland, they are part of Ireland.
Seán Óg Ó hAilpín, GAA star

Questions

1 What is meant by the phrase 'Show Racism the Red Card'?
2 Why, do you think, does this organisation use high-profile football and sports stars to educate young people?
3 Look at the poster above. What football team appears on it?

When I got racism as a kid, talking about it helped. My family educated me, my Mum and my teachers helped me and taught me how to deal with it. People need to get educated, so you need to talk to people if it happens to you.
Ashley Cole, footballer

There's no place for racism at school, football or anywhere in society. It's up to all of us to work together to stamp out racism.
Andy Cole, footballer

Bullying

As a student you have the right to an education and to feel safe and secure at school. However, victims of bullying know what school life is like without that security. Bullying is '**persistent negative behaviour directed towards a particular student**'. Bullying leads to a loss of human dignity on the part of the victim.

There are a number of ways in which an individual can be bullied. There is:
- Physical bullying
- Verbal bullying
- Other types of bullying.

1. Physical bullying:
- Punching
- Pushing
- Threatening
- Kicking
- Hitting
- Taking or hiding someone's belongings.

2. Verbal bullying:
- Teasing
- Name-calling
- Making insulting comments or remarks.

3. Other types of bullying:
- Spreading rumours about someone
- Deliberately excluding someone
- Deliberately trying to embarrass someone
- Internet bullying
- Bullying by text message

The Effects of Bullying

Bullying gives rise to a loss of human dignity on the part of the victim. Its effects include:

Physical effects	Emotional effects	Academic effects
Illness	Feelings of anxiety	Poor academic performance
Aggression	Loss of confidence	Poor punctuality
Violent outbursts	Loneliness	Poor attendance at school
	Feelings of isolation	Refusal to go to school
	Depression	Dropping out of school
	Fear	
	Suicidal thoughts	

As you can see, bullying has serious consequences for the target of the bullying. Read the poem called 'Truth' on the next page. Written by Barrie Wade, it suggests that sometimes verbal bullying can be more painful and have more lasting effects than physical bullying.

What Can I Do?

Bullying deprives an individual of his or her dignity. Although bullying occurs in most schools on a daily basis, very few incidences are actually reported. Most victims don't tell someone that it is happening to them because they are afraid they will be labelled a 'rat' (a telltale), and also fear the bullying will get worse. Some victims do not tell their parents because they think they will appear 'weak' and 'unable to stick up for themselves'.

Bullying is humiliating for the victim. If you know someone who is being bullied, there are a number of things you could do to help prevent it continuing:

- Reassure the victim that it will stop
- Refuse to join in with the bullies
- Encourage the victim to talk to an adult. This could be a parent, a teacher, a class tutor or the principal
- Make friends with that person and include him or her in your group.

Truth

by Barrie Wade

Sticks and stones may break my bones
But words can also hurt me
Stones and sticks break only skin
While words are ghosts that haunt me.
Slant and curved the word swords fall
To pierce and stick inside me
Bats and bricks may ache through bones
But words can mortify me.
Pain from words has left its scar
On mind and heart that's tender
Cuts and bruises now have healed
Its words that I remember.

> **Make a list of some other ways in which you can help victims of bullying**

Anti-Bullying Charter

One way of trying to prevent instances of bullying in your class is to draw up a class anti-bullying charter. Get into pairs or groups and come up with some ways in which bullying can be prevented in your class. As a class, agree on 10 items to be included in your class charter. Start your charter like this:

Our Anti-Bullying Charter

We, Class _____ of _____ school recognise that bullying causes a loss of human dignity. As a class we agree to the following 10 items.

1. _____
2. _____
3. _____
4. _____
5. _____

6. _____
7. _____
8. _____
9. _____
10. _____

Questions

1. What is bullying?
2. Name and describe the three types of bullying. Which type do you think is the most hurtful? Why?
3. Describe five effects of bullying.
4. Reread the poem 'Truth' by Barrie Wade.
   (i) According to the author what is the most hurtful type of bullying?
   (ii) What is meant by the phrases 'words are ghosts that haunt me' and 'word swords fall'?
5. Compose your own poem or short story on bullying.

> **IMAGINE!**
> Imagine you witnessed a classmate of yours being bullied. What actions would you take? Explain why.

3.1

1. Conduct a bullying survey in your school to investigate how many students have been bullied.

2. Celebrate International Day Against Racism in your school. You could:
→ Organise an anti-racism poster competition
→ Put on a play on the issue of racism
→ Invite someone from an immigrant organisation into your school to discuss with the students how racist behaviour effects them on an individual level, and what the cost is in terms of human dignity.

SKILLS YOU MIGHT USE:
→ Artistic   → Letter-writing   → Communication   → Public relations
→ Drama   → Telephone   → Questioning   → Survey design
→ Hosting   → Surveying   → Information gathering   → Analysis.

Can you think of other skills you may need to undertake this action?

Wordsearch on Human Dignity

```
D X Y N U G I M M T E Q N N X Z K P U M
Z I F G E B A I R J D H O Y M L B R E P
X I S N S F O A A Q T I R E F U G E E L
H H D A P P V B R K T L Y Y J R D J A C
U E B V B E L N N A L U E X Q L B U C O
R H S V L I X Y N R E C U G O U J D W T
P J B L A F L I S T E R E O T Y P I N G
E S E B Q M M I S E D U T I T T A C E N
R R M I F I R P T Z K O N M M F J E R P
U E Y Y R Y Y G P Y N V Y D O E X H C T
W X G C P T N R N M A T H E F D A O P N
Q Z S R I I F W A I P B U K Q L S G E X
A I O N N L I S D C Y E N Z X N Y B U F
D H G P V A O I K U I L X T C I L U B S
V I G A B U R M F Z S S L H H I U X B H
D Z J T C Q S S E C C A M U Y M M O K B
K J R P T E O P L O K P F L B H N X D I
B L E J T A S C S C Z I L Z L U W R S X
R V N A B Z T S E C Z M R K F R P G V N
I O S Q D F U N K W R P Y X S I O V Z O
```

■ ACCESS   ■ DIGNITY   ■ GENDER   ■ STEREOTYPING
■ ASYLUM   ■ DISABILITY   ■ PREJUDICE   ■ TRAVELLER
■ ATTITUDES   ■ DISCRIMINATION   ■ RACISM
■ BULLYING   ■ EQUALITY   ■ REFUGEE

Our Community

Three Case Studies on Human Dignity

Case Study 1

The Homeless Community

There are over 5,000 people homeless in the Republic of Ireland today. Being homeless means much more than not having a roof over your head. Being homeless means that you are deprived of security, stability, safety and a sense of belonging. Three categories of homelessness have been identified in Ireland – the **visible**, the **hidden** and those **at risk** of homelessness.

1. The Visible Homeless
These are the people who can be seen sleeping rough in doorways or on the street. These men and women might live in temporary forms of emergency accommodation – hostels and night shelters.

2. The Hidden Homeless
These are people who share accommodation with friends or family, because they have no home of their own.

3. People at Risk of Homelessness
This category includes people who currently have a home but are at risk of becoming homeless because of money problems, domestic violence, drug or alcohol misuse or some other reason.

Why Do People Become Homeless?

There are a wide variety of reasons why people become homeless. The most common reasons include:

- Family breakdown
- Unemployment
- Inadequate wages
- Alcohol misuse
- Drug misuse
- Physical or mental illness
- High house prices
- Lack of local authority housing and long waiting lists
- Leaving institutional care (when people who have spent a long time in foster care, orphanages, prisons or mental hospitals leave them, they often have nowhere to go)
- Domestic abuse and violence.

Questions

1. Approximately how many people are homeless in Ireland?
2. Name and describe the three categories of homelessness.
3. List five reasons why people can become homeless.

The Effects of Homelessness

Homelessness is an increasing problem in Ireland. It is not only adults who are affected by this problem. It is estimated that there are about 500 children who are homeless in Ireland.

Being homeless can have serious consequences:

- Having no address – without a permanent address the homeless find it difficult to apply for a job and may have problems availing of health and social services
- Having no address can mean loss of contact with friends and other valuable relationships
- Having little privacy
- Having nowhere to wash or go to the toilet
- No sense of belonging
- Feelings of isolation
- Being exposed to adverse weather conditions
- Increased likelihood of various illnesses
- A lack of safety and security
- Turning to alcohol or drugs for escape
- Feelings of depression or mental anguish which, in turn, can lead to severe mental health problems and possibly suicidal thoughts.

PHOTOCALL

Being homeless can strip an individual of his or her human dignity. Many homeless people are reported as feeling of low self-worth, isolated and alone. In the following extract, **Fr Peter McVerry**, a man who has worked relentlessly for the homeless, outlines the effects of homelessness on a young man.

A young man threw himself into the river about two weeks ago. He was pulled out and brought to hospital. The hospital kept him in, as he was suffering from severe depression. This young man was homeless. Some nights he got a bed in a hostel, most nights the hostels were all full and he slept on the street. During the day, he walked the streets, bored, tired and hungry. While he was in hospital I went to visit him. He told me: 'I can't go on living like this anymore'. 'Living like what?' I said. 'I can't go on living' he said, 'knowing that nobody cares'.

This young man almost lost his life, not from lack of food or the cold or an illness brought on by living on the streets. He almost lost his life because he had lost his dignity. He felt his life was of no value to anyone, that he was worthless, that he wasn't worth caring about. He felt useless – that really whether he lived or died would make no difference to the world or anyone in it. His sense of his own worth was destroyed, that whether he lived or died didn't even make a difference to himself.

(From *Homelessness in Ireland* by Peter McVerry. Source www.soulsearching.org)

The Department of the Environment, Heritage and Local Government and the Department of Health and Children have the responsibility to ensure that the needs of people who are homeless are met in the Republic of Ireland. There are many voluntary organisations that work in Ireland with the local authorities and the Health Service Executive to provide services for people who are homeless.

The Work of Focus Ireland

Focus Ireland is a voluntary agency that was set up in 1985 by Sister Stanislaus Kennedy, to respond to the needs of individuals or families who have found themselves homeless. Focus Ireland believes that every person has a right to a place they call home. The main work of Focus Ireland includes:

1 Providing emergency, short-term and long-term accommodation for the homeless or those at risk of becoming homeless.
2 Providing a range of services such as advice, information centres and low-cost meals.
3 Campaigning and lobbying for the rights of the homeless and for the prevention of homelessness.

Focus Ireland relies on fundraising and volunteers to keep its services going. Other organisations that work with the homeless in Ireland include:

- Simon Community
- St Vincent de Paul
- Threshold
- The Salvation Army.

ART ACTIVITY

Design a poster to highlight awareness of the effects of homelessness on individuals.

Questions

1 List some of the effects of homelessness on an individual.
2 Reread the extract written by Fr Peter McVerry. Why do you think the young man in the story lost his human dignity?
3 Write a paragraph on the work of Focus Ireland.
4 Look at the photograph below and answer the questions that follow.

a. According to the poster, why do people become homeless?
b. What organisation is responsible for this poster?
c. Why, do you think, was cardboard used as a background for this poster?
d. Can you think of one action which your class could undertake to raise money for homeless charities? Describe how your class would carry out that action.

Case Study 2

The Traveller Community

The Traveller community is a distinct ethnic group in Ireland with its own unique culture, history, traditions and values. Travellers are distinct from the settled community in that many of them lead a nomadic way of life. This lifestyle often means that members of the Traveller community have no access to basic needs such as water, sanitation and electricity. This can have an impact on the health of Travellers.

There are about 25,000 Travellers living in Ireland at present and, because they are a minority group, many have been victims of prejudice and discrimination. Some have been harassed and verbally abused. Others have been refused access to services. A recent survey by the Irish Traveller Movement found that:

- 90% of Travellers went to the pub
- 77% were told to leave the pub by a member of staff
- 79% had been refused a drink
- 80% had been refused entry because they were Travellers.

Another survey conducted by the Irish government (Know Racism, 2004) found that 72% of settled people did not want members of the Traveller community living amongst them.

Both surveys suggest that Travellers experience high levels of discrimination in Irish society, resulting in a loss of human dignity.

Fact!
→ **Life expectancy is lower for members of the Traveller community.**
→ **Traveller men live on average 10 years less than settled men.**
→ **Traveller women live on average 12 years less than settled women.**

The Irish Traveller Movement

Set up in 1990, the Irish Traveller Movement (**ITM**) is a national network of organisations working within and for the Traveller community in Ireland. This movement consists of a partnership between the Traveller and settled communities who are committed to seeking equality for Travellers in Irish society. The ITM campaigns for four key issues:

1. Accommodation
2. Equality
3. Education
4. Legal issues

This organisation also seeks to promote the participation and visibility of the Traveller community in Ireland.

Questions

1 What key issues does the ITM campaign for?
2 Do you think that the Traveller community has full equality in Irish society? Explain your answer.
3 Design and draw a poster to promote the rights of the Traveller community. Come up with a slogan and image.

FIND OUT!

Find out about these organisations that work with members of the Traveller community:
- Pavee Point
- Exchange House

Case Study
3

The Refugee Community

Imagine being forced to flee your home at a moment's notice. If you stay, your life will be in serious danger. You have just enough time to gather your family together and grab some basic provisions. You must leave behind the home that holds many memories for you and the personal possessions you have built up over the years. You don't know if you will ever come back.

Unfortunately, this scenario has been experienced by tens of thousands of refugees throughout the world.

A refugee is an individual who has been forced to flee his or her home for fear of persecution for reasons of religion, race, nationality, political opinion or membership of a particular group. Many seek safety in another country.

Why do refugees leave their homes?
Every day thousands of people leave their homes and become refugees for the following reasons:

■ **War** – War forces many people to leave their homes because they fear for their lives.

■ **Natural disasters** – Natural disasters such as hurricanes, earthquakes and storms can force people to leave their homes.

■ **Political reasons** – Some countries, especially developing countries, are ruled by governments that are corrupt. These governments introduce policies and measures that discriminate against various individuals and groups and deny them their basic human rights.

■ **Economic reasons** – Some people leave their homes because they have a poor standard of living and are paid a low wage. They look for a better life in a more prosperous country.

An **asylum seeker** is an individual who seeks to be recognised as a refugee in another country, but who is waiting for his or her claim for asylum (safety) to be processed. This process can take many years.

Questions

1 What is a refugee?
2 What is an asylum seeker?
3 Name and describe two reasons why refugees leave their homes.

Babik's Story

Babik is a Turkish Kurd who was persecuted in his own country becuase of his political views. His family smuggled him out of Turkey to Ireland. He applied for refugee status and the Irish government has allowed him to stay on humanitarian grounds. Babik works as a builder around Dublin where he lives. "I enjoy working in Ireland but I often get paid less than Irish builders. Most of my workmates are nice but a few do not like me. They say I am stopping Irish people getting jobs. I am just trying to earn a living and pay my taxes like everybody else. I love living and working in Ireland but I miss my family and friends back in Turkey. I wish I could return there some day.

Questions

1 Why did Babik leave his own country?
2 Has Babik suffered a loss of human dignity in Ireland. Explain your answer.
3 What problems has Babik encountered since he arrived in Ireland?

YOU DECIDE

Imagine that you live in an African state. A neighbour has just told you that gunfire has broken out 500 metres from your home. You are advised to leave immediately. The only way out is to flee on foot to a refugee camp 50 miles away. You can only bring three items from the list below. What items will you take? Give reasons for your choices.

→ Passport
→ Clothes
→ Money
→ Water
→ Blankets
→ Photographs
→ Food
→ Medicine

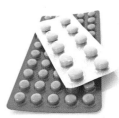

SHUTTERSTOCK

Refugees and Asylum Seekers in Ireland

Over the last decade Ireland has become a multicultural society. This means that there are people living and working in Ireland from many other cultures and countries. One reason for this has been the increase in the number of asylum seekers coming to Ireland, seeking recognition of their refugee status. (Legally, however, asylum seekers are not allowed to work until their case comes up and they are accepted as refugees. The alternative is deportation back to the country from which they fled.)

In 2008 the top five countries of origin of asylum seekers coming to Ireland were:

1 Nigeria   3 Iraq   5 Georgia
2 Pakistan   4 China

There is a general misconception that Ireland is being 'flooded' with asylum seekers. Less than 1% of the world's refugees come to Ireland. The following table illustrates the actual numbers of asylum seekers who have travelled to Ireland in recent years.

1994	1995	1996	1997	1998	1999	2000
362	424	1,179	3,883	4,626	7,724	10,938

2001	2002	2003	2004	2005	2006	2007	2008
10,325	11,624	7,900	4,766	4,323	4,314	3,985	3,866

Exploding the Myth – Facts about Asylum Seekers

Many people in Irish society are misinformed about the entitlements of asylum seekers. They think that all asylum seekers are housed in luxurious accommodation and receive generous allowances. In reality:

■ Since 2000, asylum seekers receive **direct provision** from the State. This means that they are housed in communal accommodation centres throughout Ireland. For example, the former amusement park, Mosney, outside Balbriggan, now houses 7,000 asylum seekers who are waiting for their applications to be processed. Each asylum seeker receives three meals a day. Over 50% of asylum seekers have been in direct provision for between 9 and 24 months. Around 7% have lived in accommodation centres for over two years

■ Because they are housed in these accommodation centres and their meals are provided directly, asylum seekers receive **reduced social welfare payments**:
  – An adult receives €19.10 per week
  – A child receives €9.60 per week.

■ Child benefit **is not paid** to asylum seekers who arrived in Ireland after May 2004

- Adult asylum seekers are **not permitted** to work

- Adult asylum seekers are **not permitted** to partake in educational or training courses

- Children seeking asylum are entitled to receive primary and secondary level education. On leaving secondary education, they **cannot access** third level education or post-Leaving Certificate courses, nor are they entitled to maintenance grants from local authorities.

Questions

1 Why, do you think, are so many Irish people misinformed about refugees and asylum seekers in Ireland?
2 Are you surprised by the facts on the entitlements of asylum seekers? Why?
3 Do you think that the rights of asylum seekers are fully realised in Ireland? Give a reason for your answer.
4 Do you think that asylum seekers in Ireland suffer a loss of human dignity? Give reasons for your answer.

The Irish Refugee Council

The Irish Refugee Council, set up in 1992, is a voluntary non-governmental organisation that promotes the interests of refugees and asylum seekers in Ireland. The main aims of this organisation are:

1. To ensure that Ireland's policies concerning refugees and asylum seekers fully respect international law and the rights of refugees and asylum seekers.
2. To promote public awareness and an understanding of refugees and asylum seekers.
3. To provide information and advice on the rights and entitlements of refugees and asylum seekers.

DATE TO REMEMBER! International Refugee Day – 20th June

Ideas For Taking Action 3.2

1. Guest speakers:
→ A Traveller
→ A member of a Traveller organisation
→ A homeless person
→ A member of a homeless organisation
→ A refugee or asylum seeker
→ A member of an organisation that promotes the interests of refugees or asylum seekers.

2. A visit to:
→ A halting site
→ A homeless shelter
→ Asylum seeker accommodation.

SKILLS YOU MIGHT USE:
→ Telephone   → Financial   → Questioning
→ Letter-writing   → Teamwork   → Public relations.
→ Organisation   → Listening

Can you think of other skills you may need to undertake this action?

The State's Role in Upholding Human Dignity

Ireland has become a multicultural society so it is important that all people living in Ireland can live their lives with dignity. To ensure that everyone is treated equally and that everyone's human rights are protected, the government has put in place a number of laws and measures to ensure that no individual is deliberately discriminated against. In Ireland the **Minister for Justice, Equality and Law Reform** is responsible for the protection of human rights. Can you name the current Minister for Justice, Equality and Law Reform?

The Equal Status Acts 2000 and 2004

The Equal Status Acts are a series of laws that protect the rights and uphold the dignity of individuals. These laws were introduced in order to promote equality and reduce victimisation, harassment and certain forms of discrimination. In addition, these laws require reasonable accommodation to be given to those with disabilities.

These laws apply to people who:
- Buy and sell a wide variety of **goods**
- Use or provide a wide range of **services** (e.g. banks, places of entertainment, transport)
- Obtain or dispose of **accommodation**
- Attend or are in charge of **educational establishments**.

This act also prohibits discrimination on the following nine grounds:
- Gender
- Marital status
- Family status
- Sexual orientation
- Religion
- Age
- Disability
- Race
- Membership of the Traveller community

Under the Equal Status Act, persons who feel that they have been victimised, harassed or discriminated against in some way may make a claim to the **Equality Tribunal**. This body investigates, hears and decides on claims under this Act.

The Equality Authority

Set up in 1999, the Equality Authority provides information on the Equal Status Acts to the general public. It provides advice and assistance to those who feel they have been discriminated against on one of the nine grounds of discrimination. In addition, the authority may also provide legal assistance to people who make a claim under the Equal Status Acts.

Irish Human Rights Commission

Set up in 2001, the Irish Human Rights Commission (IHRC) is an organisation that aims to strengthen the protection of human rights in Ireland. This organisation, funded by the government, ensures that the rights of all people living in Ireland are fully realised and protected in both policy and practice. It also sees to it that the Irish government upholds all the European and international agreements it has made. This commission further provides recommendations to the government on various human rights issues.

Questions

1 Why were the Equal Status Acts introduced?
2 Who does the law apply to?
3 What are the nine grounds of discrimination?
4 In your own words, describe the role of the Equality Authority.
5 Why was the IHRC set up?

The Ombudsman for Children

Emily Logan

The Irish government also has a responsibility to protect and promote the rights of children as children are some the most vulnerable members of society. To safeguard the rights and welfare of children and to give everyone under the age of 18 a voice, the Ombudsman for Children office was established in 2002. Emily Logan was the first Ombudsman for children in Ireland. She worked as a nurse for 22 years so she had lots of experience of working with children and young people.

The three main areas of work outlined in the Ombudsman for Children Act, 2002, are:
■ Promoting children's rights
■ Research and policy
■ Complaints and investigations.

Children can make complaints through the Ombudsman if they feel they have been treated unfairly by government departments, for example hospitals.

Questions

1 Who became the first Ombudsman for Children in Ireland?
2 What Act established this office?
3 What are the main aims of the Ombudsman for Children?
4 List the three main areas of work outlined in the Ombudsman for Children Act 2002.

Ideas For Taking Action   3.3

1. Invite a member of the Equality Authority, the Irish Human Rights Commission or the Ombudsman for Children to your class to find out more about the laws that uphold human dignity in Ireland.

SKILLS YOU MIGHT USE:

→ Telephone
→ Letter-writing
→ Communication.

→ Organisation
→ Teamwork

Can you think of other skills you may need to undertake this action?

An International Case Study in Human Dignity: Child Labour

CHAPTER 3.4

Case Study

Child Labour

Child labour can be defined as any work done by **children under the age of 18** that is damaging to their physical, emotional and social development. The majority of child labourers are denied the right of full-time education.

There are approximately 218 million children engaged in full-time work in the world today. About 14% of all children between 5 and 17 years old are child labourers. This means that 1 in 7 children is a child labourer. In some cases children as young as 4 or 5 work full-time.

CAMERAPRESS

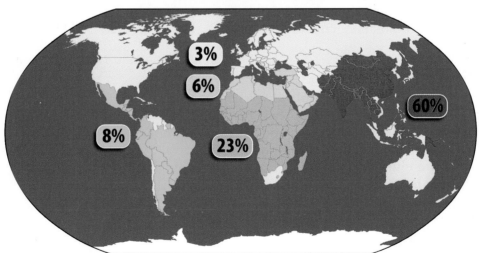

- → **60% of child labourers come from Asia and the Pacific regions**
- → **23% come from sub-Saharan Africa**
- → **8% come from Latin America and the Caribbean**
- → **6% come from North Africa and the Middle East**
- → **3% come from Europe, Russia and North America**

As you can see from the map above, most child labourers come from developing countries where many families are caught in a vicious cycle of poverty. Children often provide essential income for these families.

What Do Child Labourers Work At?

Throughout the world, child labourers are engaged in many forms of work. Some of their jobs include:

- Making rugs and carpets
- Making footballs and footwear
- Mining
- Child soldiers
- Domestic servants
- Farming and fishing
- Making fireworks and matches
- Making bricks and doing general construction work.

Many children are subjected to long hours in unhealthy and unsafe working conditions. Despite this, they are often paid very little for their work. Many children are afraid to speak up about their conditions in case they lose their jobs or are beaten by their employers.

Why Are Young Children Employed?

There are a number of reasons why people engage the labour of young children:

1 Children are often encouraged to work by their families because they live in extreme poverty. The money earned by young children can help their families to buy the basic necessities to live.

2 Employers do not have to pay children as much as adults. Employing children increases their profit margins.

3 Many children who work are often uneducated. This means they are unaware of employment laws and workers' rights.

Bonded Labour

Some children are engaged in **bonded labour**. When parents are unable to repay loans or debts, the creditor can exploit the situation by using the child's labour to pay off the loan. Many families are uneducated and cannot calculate the interest payments. As a result a child is often tricked or trapped into working as a bonded labourer for many years.

CAMERA PRESS

Bonded labour is one of the most common means of slavery in the modern world. Children work for long hours, often seven days a week, for little or no wages.

Despite the fact that bonded labour is illegal in many of the countries where it occurs, most governments are unwilling to enforce the law and often turn a blind eye to this deplorable practice.

Questions

1 List three reasons why children are employed in developing countries.
2 What is bonded labour?
3 Describe briefly the working conditions that many child workers have to endure.

The following is a case file of one bonded labourer. Dilip from India became a bonded labourer because his family was unable to repay a debt. Study the case file and answer the questions that follow.

India: Carpet Knotting/Bonded Labour
DILIP KUMAR

Name:	Dilip Kumar
Age:	14
Exploited since:	1988 (5 years old)
Sold for:	50 Rps (77 cents)
Liberated on:	25 October 1995
Organisation:	Bachapan Bachao Andolan
Project:	Mukti Ashram, Delhi
Place of birth:	Kalabalua
Region:	district Purnia (Bihar)
Country:	India
Adopted by:	ChildRight Worldwide

WORKING CONDITIONS:

First owner:	Kariya Bind
Second owner:	Rajendra Sing
	Kurmaicha, Gopiganj in Bhadohi
Type of work:	Carpet weaving
Working hours:	4 a.m.: getting up
	4 to 5 a.m.: morning routine work
	5 to 8 a.m.: carpet weaving
	8 a.m.: breakfast (watery rice)
	8.15 to 1 p.m.: weaving
	1 to 1.30 p.m.: lunch
	1.30 to 9 p.m.: weaving
	9 p.m.: dinner
	9.30 to 11.00 p.m.: carpet weaving
Days off:	None
Wage:	None (bonded labour)
Education:	None

GENERAL CHARACTERISTICS OF CHILD SLAVERY:

1. Forced labour
2. Extreme working hours
3. Lack of sleep/exhaustion
4. No or little wage
5. No free time
6. No education
7. No possessions
8. No privacy
9. No freedom of movement
10. No sick leave/health care
11. Malnutrition
12. Emotional isolation
13. Corporal punishment
14. Arbitrary assault
15. Sexual abuse
16. Extremely high mortality rate

POSED BY MODEL

HEALTH REPORT UPON LIBERATION:

Severe anaemic (haemoglobin 04.5% on 31st October 1995) - malnutrition - lack of appetite - hepatomegaly - slight - increased serum bilirubin - oedema in leg and on face - malignant pustule on skin - allergic dermatitis - fungal infection of genitalia - malena - burning under sternum - night blindness - stomatitis, white tongue, inflammation of gums and white pigmentation on inner surface of lower lip (due to tobacco chewing) - increased E.S.R. - allergic rhinitis.

Questions

1 How many years had Dilip been enslaved?
2 How much was he sold for?
3 Describe a typical working day.
4 How much was Dilip paid for his work?
5 What medical conditions did Dilip develop as a result of his enslavement?
6 How did Dilip escape from his enslavement?

FACT!

There are around 20 million slaves throughout the world today.

School is the Best Place to Work – Campaigning Against Child Labour

School is the Best Place to Work is a campaign that seeks to eliminate all forms of child labour through providing full-time, quality education. This international campaign is backed by Concern, an Irish voluntary organisation that promotes the rights of people worldwide. This campaign calls on international governments to:

1. Eliminate child labour through the provision of full-time education for all children up to 14 years of age.

2. Ensure that EU members allocate at least 8% of overseas development aid to education in developing countries.

3. Ensure that girls and young children from vulnerable groups are integrated into the formal education system.

Questions

The above poster marks World Day Against Child Labour which takes place on 12th June each year. Study the poster and answer the questions that follow.
1 What is the central message of this poster?
2 What organisation is responsible for this poster?
3 Briefly describe one action your class could undertake to mark World Day Against Child Labour in your school?

3.4

1. Raise awareness about the issue of child labour. Possible actions might include:

→ Organise a petition against child labour
→ Make some anti-child labour posters for your school
→ Lobby politicians about the issue
→ Write letters to businesses that employ child labourers.

2. Invite a guest speaker from Concern or one of the other children's organisations to find out more about the issue of child labour.

SKILLS YOU MIGHT USE:

→ Letter-writing   → Petition design
→ Telephone   → Surveying
→ Communication   → Public relations.

Can you think of other skills that you may need to undertake this action?

Wordsearch on Human Dignity

L	Y	N	E	D	J	R	D	R	Q	E	E	Y	T	I	N	G	I	D	I
P	O	T	Q	Q	E	J	E	K	P	N	C	M	E	R	V	Y	V	E	Y
L	B	S	I	F	U	L	C	G	L	M	I	U	I	E	Z	W	I	P	C
Z	B	R	U	L	L	A	J	E	U	O	D	L	R	S	L	I	F	J	X
V	I	G	E	E	I	W	L	V	S	D	U	Y	F	P	M	G	G	R	V
B	E	P	V	X	T	B	X	I	Q	F	J	S	R	E	R	W	B	Y	R
E	N	A	J	H	D	V	A	L	T	J	E	A	J	C	E	W	W	O	T
Y	R	Q	N	I	A	E	B	S	M	Y	R	H	H	T	B	T	Z	C	L
T	I	I	F	T	T	J	F	O	I	C	P	E	P	G	Q	P	W	E	V
J	W	P	P	D	M	J	R	V	H	D	P	J	X	D	F	G	H	X	N
Z	O	A	N	Y	S	O	X	I	W	Y	C	W	R	T	E	L	U	I	G
C	J	F	H	O	M	E	L	E	S	S	U	J	J	M	E	K	Z	B	K
T	D	Q	W	Z	W	D	L	X	D	Y	P	D	I	Y	S	H	R	I	G
O	L	L	W	B	L	W	M	B	S	R	G	I	L	E	Z	I	S	Q	N
G	J	O	J	A	A	G	X	Y	Y	B	W	V	Z	U	J	U	C	H	X
J	Z	C	B	H	U	F	I	H	G	V	V	V	J	F	O	D	G	A	L
K	H	O	E	P	Y	T	O	E	R	E	T	S	D	D	P	I	J	N	R
I	U	P	P	B	M	D	E	V	V	N	A	N	G	W	K	Q	L	Z	F
R	U	O	E	K	K	L	P	T	N	Z	S	R	B	L	F	Q	C	Q	R
K	R	T	I	V	K	S	C	V	X	X	P	A	V	M	X	M	H	U	C

■ ASYLUM   ■ EQUALITY   ■ REFUGEE
■ CHILDLABOUR   ■ HOMELESS   ■ RESPECT
■ DIGNITY   ■ PREJUDICE   ■ STEREOTYPE
■ DISABILITY   ■ RACISM   ■ TRAVELLER

Crossword on Human Dignity

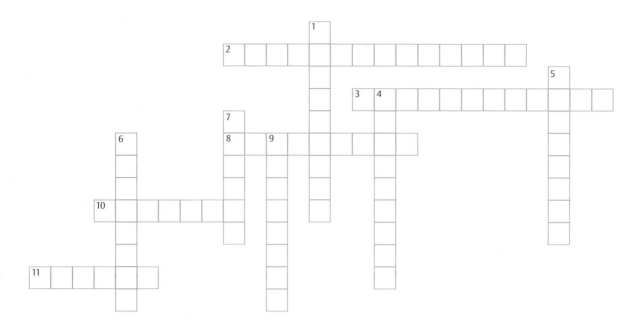

Across

2 This occurs when we treat someone differently or unfairly.

3 This happens when we label someone.

8 This person upholds the rights of children in Ireland.

10 A person forced to flee their home.

11 The idea that some races are better than others.

Down

1 When we prejudge an individual or a group.

4 This community lead a nomadic way of life.

5 Not able bodied

6 Without a home.

7 When a child's labour is used to repay a debt.

9 Name-calling is one example of this behaviour.

Word bank

- → BULLYING
- → BONDED
- → RACISM
- → DISCRIMINATION
- → TRAVELLER
- → DISABLED
- → HOMELESS
- → STEREOTYPING
- → OMBUDSMAN
- → PREJUDICE
- → REFUGEE

Human Dignity - Past Examination Questions

1 Below are the names of six groups of people and logos of six organisations with which they are closely linked. In the space provided beneath each logo, write the name of the group of people with which it is most closely linked.

You may write only **ONE** name under each logo. You may use the name of each group only **ONCE**.

Groups of people

Asylum seekers and refugees

Homeless people

Older people

People who face the death penalty

Poor people

The Traveller community

a. Group of people

_____

b. Group of people

_____

c. Group of people

_____

d. Group of people

_____

e. Group of people

_____

f. Group of people

_____

(CSPE Paper, 2007)

2 Mobile Phone Bullying

Texting is a great way to stay in touch with your friends and family but sadly it can also be used to bully, harass and frighten people. Text bullying can be texts that frighten, insult, threaten you or make you feel uncomfortable. Your CSPE class has decided to do some work on this issue.

(a) Write a short article for your school newsletter in which you give **THREE** pieces of advice about what students should do if they receive a bullying text message.
(b) Name an Action Project that **YOUR CSPE CLASS** could undertake on this issue and describe **THREE** tasks your class would do as part of this action.
(c) Name and describe **THREE** other actions that **YOUR SCHOOL** could take to help prevent text bullying in your school.

(CSPE Exam Paper, 2009)

Website Watch
Check out the following websites that can give you more information on the concept of human dignity.

www.theredcard.ie
www.disability-federation.ie
www.paveepoint.ie
www.focusireland.ie

www.irishrefugeecouncil.ie
www.oco.ie
www.stopchildlabour.net
www.trocaire.org

TAKING ACTION

A Bullying Survey in My School

A survey is an ideal way of finding out about the attitudes of others on various issues. Surveys can also give you valuable insights about various issues in your communities.

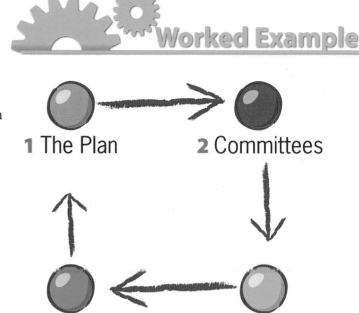

1 The Plan → **2** Committees

4 Review ← **3** The Survey

Worked Example

The plan:
Who will we survey?
How many will we survey?
What information do we need to find out?
How long will the survey take to fill out?
How and when will we survey?
Do we need to pilot the survey?

Committees:
What committees do we need?
What are the responsibilities of each committee?
How will we assign students to each committee?

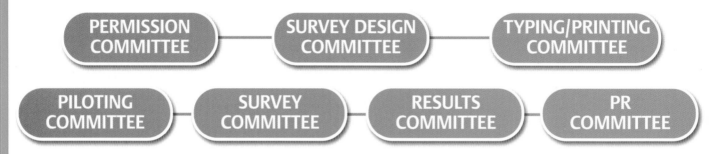

PERMISSION COMMITTEE — SURVEY DESIGN COMMITTEE — TYPING/PRINTING COMMITTEE

PILOTING COMMITTEE — SURVEY COMMITTEE — RESULTS COMMITTEE — PR COMMITTEE

Can you think of any other committees you might need for this action?

The survey:
Carry out the survey.

The review:
Was the action successful? Why or why not?
Would you do anything differently?
What did you find out?
Did you find out at least five new pieces of information about bullying?
Were you surprised by your findings?
Has this action given you a better insight into the issue of bullying?

Skills You Might Use:

→ Survey design
→ Interviewing
→ Computer
→ Typing
→ Analysing
→ Listening.

Stewardship

The fundamental idea of stewardship is that we are all responsible for the care of our planet. No one person owns any part of this planet – we should all be active in caring for and maintaining it. If we do not act to protect our planet, there is a danger that future generations will not have the same opportunities as we have had to enjoy nature. It is up to each one of us to be **stewards** of our environment.

The Individual as Steward of the Planet

Human beings, like animals and plants, are a part of nature. The environment is everything that surrounds us and affects us – mountains, oceans, rivers, deserts, trees, animals, our villages, towns and cities. We have a great effect on all of these. From the moment you wake in the morning to the moment you go to bed at night you are having an **impact** on your environment. You can have a positive impact on it if you take small and simple steps to care for it. A good start is to become aware of the many environmental issues that are being talked about in Ireland and the world today.

How You Can be a Steward of the Environment

You can help your environment in many ways. There are many little things that you can do in your own house and garden to help the environment. If we all try to make these small gestures then we can make a great difference.

There are four simple yet very important ways in which we can help our environment: reduce, reuse, recycle and repair. These are called the 4 Rs.

The 4 Rs

Reduce

■ If your house needs a new appliance, encourage your family to buy an energy-efficient model

■ Use low-energy light bulbs – they will last up to ten times longer and use 70% less electricity to give the same amount of light

■ Switch off all televisions, computers and electronic items after use. Don't leave them on standby as this uses valuable energy

■ When you boil the kettle, put in only the amount of water you actually need – otherwise you are using energy needlessly

■ Run the dishwasher only when it has a full load – this saves on energy and water

■ Turn off lights in rooms that aren't being used

■ Take a shower instead of a bath – it uses 70% less water and much less energy

Reuse

■ We can make use of things such as plastic containers, envelopes and glass jars at home many times over

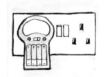

■ Where possible use rechargeable batteries instead of disposable ones

■ If you use plastic bags or containers to store your lunch, reuse them rather than disposing of them every day

■ Create a compost pile for such things as old teabags, eggshells, grass clippings, leaves and vegetable peelings. This can then be reused as garden fertiliser

Recycle

■ Do not throw out old clothes or shoes – bring them to your local charity shop

■ All aluminium cans, tin cans and glass bottles can be rinsed out and brought to your local recycling facility

■ Bring your Christmas tree to your local collection centre where it will be processed into organic mulch for gardening

■ All newspapers, brochures and leaflets can be recycled, thereby helping to reduce forest destruction

Repair

■ Repair broken appliances when possible rather than disposing of them and buying new ones

■ Repair leaks. A leaking tap can waste up to 90 litres of water a day

■ If you break the screen on your mobile or MP4, try and repair it with tape rather than rushing out to buy a new model!

■ Faulty heating systems, as well as being dangerous, can use too much energy and should be repaired immediately

What is your Carbon Number?

Each one of us has a carbon number. This is the amount of greenhouse gases we produce each year. By using energy we produce these gases. If we follow the 4Rs – Reduce, Reuse, Recycle and Repair – we can have a lower carbon number, which will help the environment.

You can discover your own carbon number and find ways to help the environment by visiting **www.change.ie**.

Group Activity	Divide the class into four groups and come up with ways in which you and your classmates could help reduce, reuse, recycle and repair in your school.

Student Task	Using the headings 'Reduce', 'Reuse', 'Recycle' and 'Repair', make a list of the ways in which you and your family could help the environment.

Wordsearch on Stewardship

R	A	I	W	M	Y	T	R	K	E	E	R	E	X	T
O	S	N	T	R	S	S	C	P	L	E	M	N	G	Q
N	J	Y	E	O	V	J	L	W	C	Q	Q	V	F	R
G	P	J	P	N	E	D	D	H	Y	R	X	I	F	E
I	D	M	L	C	E	R	A	P	C	U	O	R	W	D
C	O	A	T	Q	E	R	U	C	E	F	O	O	N	U
C	P	X	B	P	G	J	G	O	R	G	A	N	I	C
H	K	F	A	A	J	F	I	Y	O	G	A	M	P	E
X	V	I	B	D	N	P	E	S	F	M	T	E	J	K
W	R	L	D	Z	R	I	X	S	S	J	Y	N	X	M
F	E	O	Y	W	M	A	N	B	U	V	E	T	D	K
M	H	T	A	R	Z	D	W	M	H	E	B	G	F	D
T	N	E	I	C	I	F	F	E	R	A	R	N	Z	G
J	N	O	B	R	A	C	J	Q	T	Y	F	S	W	K
Z	F	I	N	L	P	E	H	U	C	S	H	E	M	F

- **CARBON**
- **COMPOST**
- **EFFICIENT**
- **ENERGY**
- **ENVIRONMENT**
- **ORGANIC**
- **RECHARGABLE**
- **RECYCLE**
- **REDUCE**
- **REPAIR**
- **REUSE**
- **STEWARD**

4.1

Celebrate Energy Awareness Week (third week in September)

You and your classmates could create energy awareness in the school. For example, you could organise a guest speaker from ENFO (information on the environment) to address pupils in the school and run a poster campaign to highlight the event.

SKILLS YOU MIGHT USE:

→ Letter-writing
→ Telephone
→ Computer
→ Communications
→ Designing a poster
→ Hosting
→ Listening

Can you think of other skills you may need to undertake this action?

Stewardship in The Community

Unfortunately, in some communities, pollution of the environment has become a very serious problem. In many parts of Ireland, there has been a massive increase in pollution levels as we have become very much a **throw-away** society. We have traditionally dumped most of our waste in **landfill sites**. These are places where all sorts of rubbish are simply buried under tons of earth. Most of the landfill sites in Ireland are almost full and need to be replaced by other more **sustainable** ways of waste disposal.

The impact of landfill sites on the environment can be serious. When waste is broken down by **bacteria**, this leads to the production of gas and chemicals. Unfortunately, occasionally the chemicals may **leach** (soak) into local water supplies and create health risks.

Many communities are active in protecting their local environment. Some groups now believe they can make a real difference to ensure that future generations will be able to enjoy the benefits of a pleasant environment. There have been many instances in the past number of years where community groups have strongly opposed plans to open new landfill sites in their locality.

Bring Bank

One way local communities can help reduce the amount of waste going to a landfill is to make use of the many **bring banks** where material suitable for recycling can be left. The following can be brought to your local bring bank:

→ **Wastepaper and cardboard** → **Green waste e.g. hedge clippings** → **Glass** → **Plastics** → **Batteries**

→ **White goods** → **DIY rubble** → **Clothes** → **Waste oils**

Incineration

Another way waste may be recycled and reused is by **incineration**. This is where waste is burned under controlled conditions. The heat created by some incinerators can be used to generate small amounts of electricity. In this way, waste is changed to energy.

There are only a small number of incinerators in Ireland. Many people do not like having them in their communities as they claim they can cause health problems.

WALKING DEBATE

Incinerators play a vital role in improving our environment.

ECO-UNESCO
Ireland's Environmental Education and Youth Organisation

eco
UNESCO
conserving the environment
empowering young people

Are you 15 to 18?
Are you concerned about Climate Change?
Then come along and join us at

ECO-UNESCO's
National Youth
ECO-Forum 2009

What's So Hot About Climate Change 2 ?
Countdown to Copenhagen

Wednesday 25 November 2009
Dublin City Centre
REGISTER TO TAKE PART TODAY!

Contact **ECO-UNESCO** for more details:
ECO-UNESCO, 26 Clare Street, Dublin 2
Tel: +353 1 662 54 91
Email: info@ecounesco.ie
www.ecounesco.ie

ECO-UNESCO is affiliated to the World Federation of UNESCO Clubs, Centres and Associations

Supported by:

Youth
Education and Culture DG
'Youth in Action' Programme

NDP

ECO-UNESCO is part-funded by the Department of Education and Science Youth Service Scheme with Support of the National Lottery Funds

Find out more about Climate Change

Voice your views

Meet the experts

Get to know other young people

Take action on Climate Change

Questions

1 Name the environmental problem mentioned in this poster.
2 Name the organisation promoting this event.
3 How could this event encourage young people to make a difference?
4 Design a poster for a campaign in your school based on the concept of stewardship.
5 Suggest a suitable slogan for the campaign.

IMAGINE

Imagine that your local council has proposed the introduction of an incinerator to reduce waste and create energy for the local area. Make a brief list of the advantages and disadvantages of having an incinerator in your community.

Kildonaghy Environmental Alliance

The residents of this community have come together to fight the local council's decision to locate a new superdump in the area. They have formed the Kildonaghy Environmental Alliance. The alliance has held two public meetings so far and has organised a meeting with local politicians to discuss the issue. The alliance feels that there are numerous reasons why a superdump should not be located here. These are some of the main ones:

- Fears of contamination of the local water supply
- Loss of local recreation space
- Potential air pollution
- Large increase in rodents and scavenging birds
- Risk of danger to the health of the local residents.

In response to these concerns, the county manager has written to the alliance and has made the following points, which she feels should help put the residents at ease:

- A layer of lining will be put at the base of the landfill site to ensure that possible contaminants do not leach into the soil and water supply
- A company will be employed to make sure rodents, such as rats, are controlled
- The local recreation space will be protected from the site and a row of trees will be planted between it and the landfill site
- Air pollution will be kept to a minimum
- The Environmental Protection Agency will inspect the site regularly and results of these inspections will be made available to local residents.

WALKING DEBATE

Organise a walking debate on the idea of locating a dump in your locality.
In your debate, deal with the issues raised in Kildonaghy and try to include other issues which may be relevant.

The Environmental Awareness Officer

There are many other environmental issues facing local communities. Most local authorities now employ an Environmental Awareness Officer to deal with these issues and to promote better management of waste in our communities. The Environmental Awareness Officer's duties include:

- Setting up recycling facilities
- Setting up the 'Green Schools' programme
- Writing information leaflets and distributing them
- Running campaigns encouraging good waste management practice
- Organising advertising campaigns.

Issue Tracking

Track an environmental issue in your local newspaper. Find out as much as you can about the issue and organise a structured class debate when you have sufficient information.

Walkabout

Organise a class walkabout around your school and its grounds to 'take in' the school environment. The walkabout is done in silence. You must use your eyes, ears and nose to investigate your school environment. In particular, be on the lookout for things that are harmful to the environment but also make a note of things that are positive.

Ideas For Taking Action

4.2

Arrange for your local Environment Awareness Officer to visit your class and tell you about the environmental issues in your locality, also the steps being taken to promote better waste management in your community.

SKILLS YOU MIGHT USE:

- → Letter-writing
- → Hosting
- → Organising
- → Negotiation
- → Questioning
- → Reporting

Can you think of other skills you may need to undertake this action?

National Issues in Stewardship

In Ireland, the government department with responsibility for stewardship of the environment is the **Department of the Environment, Heritage and Local Government**. It has a vital role to play in educating all of us citizens to become responsible stewards. The Department has traditionally been located in Dublin, but plans are in place to relocate to the south-east. The person with overall responsibility for the running of the department is the Minister.

The Minister and the Department regularly look for new ways in which to safeguard the environment. Recent measures include:

- Introducing a tax on plastic bags
- Encouraging the planting of trees
- Banning smoke-producing fuels in urban areas
- Imposing heavy fines on polluters.

The Department actively seeks to improve our environment. It intends to focus on sources of pollution or litter such as:

1 Chewing gum: This has long been a problem in urban areas. Some countries, such as South Korea, impose a tax on companies producing gum and gum products. Here in Ireland, the cost of cleaning gum from our streets has risen dramatically. If a tax is **levied** (put on) on chewing gum, then this would help pay for the cleaning costs.

2 Fast-food packaging: Countries such as Japan and Taiwan have introduced taxes on plastic food packaging, plastic cups and cutlery. In Ireland we use large amounts of these and they are putting a great strain on our environment. It seems that the only way to get fast food producers to cut back on these is to introduce a tax on them.

3 ATM Receipts: When people use ATM machines, they often just drop their receipts on the street. The cost of cleaning up this litter is met by local authorities and not the banks. Is this fair? Many people believe that it is not and that the banks should ensure that their customers dispose of their receipts responsibly.

The Green Schools Programme

PHOTOCALL 3. SHUTTERSTOCK 1

The Department of the Environment, Heritage and Local Government is aware that the best time in which citizens can learn about the value of protecting their environment is when they are in school. An agency which works for the Department is **An Taisce** and it runs a very successful programme for schools throughout the country called the **Green Schools Programme**. It was launched in 1997 and around 500 schools have now received a Green Flag for actively protecting and improving their environment.

Group Activity Divide the class into five groups. Each group must come up with a list of five simple actions that could make a difference to the school and reduce the school's carbon number.

Protecting Nature in Ireland

It is wonderful to think that we share our country with 28 species of land mammals, 400 species of birds, over 4,000 plant species and more than 12,000 species of insects! However, if we do not take our role as stewards seriously many of these species will disappear from our countryside.

Humans are constantly putting animals, plants, birds and insects in danger by doing as they wish to the environment. Fortunately there are areas of the country where wildlife is being looked after (**conserved**) by the Department of the Environment, Heritage and Local Government. These areas are called **National Parks** and there are six of them in Ireland:

- Killarney National Park, Co. Kerry
- Wicklow Mountains National Park, Co. Wicklow
- Glenveagh National Park, Co. Donegal
- The Burren National Park, Co. Clare
- Connemara National Park, Co. Galway
- Ballycoy National Park, Co. Mayo.

The Burren National Park, Co Clare

PHOTOCALL 2

The Burren National Park is a very special place and attracts many visitors every year. It has some of the most unusual plant life in Ireland. Plants that are not found anywhere else in the country grow in the Burren for example some that are normally found in the Alps and the Mediterranean.

There are also many rare species of animals, insects and birds found in the Burren, such as pine martens and wild goats, along with butterflies which are unique to the park. The landscape of the Burren is also stunning, containing beautiful sites such as the Ailwee Caves and the Cliffs of Moher.

However, the beauty of the Burren National Park could be a major problem in itself. If too many people visit the park and do not respect the environment when visiting, then many of these rare species may be destroyed. It is the job of the National Parks and Wildlife Service to protect against this danger of **extinction**.

Student Task A local developer has proposed building a hotel and leisure centre close to the Burren. Describe the reaction of a local Green Party politician to the proposal – you may do this in the form of a letter to the local newspaper.

The Importance of Trees to our Environment

Ireland has very little tree cover in comparison with other European countries. Only 10% of our land is covered by trees compared with an average of 30% for the rest of Europe. This might not seem like a major problem, but when you examine trees in detail you will find that they play a key role in our environment. Their benefits include:

- Producing food for wildlife
- Protecting soil from erosion
- Providing a habitat for plants, animals, birds and insects
- Adding valuable nutrients to the soil
- Absorbing pollutants from the atmosphere.

The Green Party

This is the one political party in Ireland which places a major emphasis on stewardship and protection of the environment. The party was founded in 1981 by Christopher Fettes. It became a government party for the first time in 2007.

Two of its TDs – John Gormley and Eamon Ryan – became the first Green Party ministers in an Irish government. The Green Party believes that, as stewards of the planet, we have a duty to pass it on in a clean and healthy state to future generations. Some of its policies are:

- Reducing the amount of waste dumped in landfills
- Resisting superdumps
- Finding alternatives to incineration as a solution to waste management
- Being against nuclear power in Ireland
- Requiring all citizens to separate waste so that recycling and composting become part of the way we all manage waste
- Passing legislation to make sure agriculture and industry produce less waste.

> **WALKING DEBATE**
> Irish people do not care for their environment.

> Can you name the current leader of the Green Party?

> **RESEARCH ACTIVITY**
>
> Contact An Taisce to find out more about the Green Schools Programme. Maybe your school is already a Green School, but if not, then why not become one?

Ideas For Taking Action 4.3

Organise your class to plant some native Irish trees in your school grounds or in your local community. Try and get the local media to highlight the event. This could be done during National Tree week in March. By doing this, you will be helping to increase native species in your area. The trees you plant will also absorb pollutants from the air!

SKILLS YOU MIGHT USE:

→ Communication
→ Organisation
→ Negotiating
→ Public relations
→ Fundraising
→ Planning

Can you think of other skills you may need to undertake this action?

Stewardship – The International Connection

Our planet is a very fragile place and we are putting a lot of pressure on it. The past 300 years of industrial activity have been very damaging to it. We have been slowly choking the planet by polluting its air, soil and water.

Climate Change

Since the middle of the 1700s (the industrial revolution), humans have been burning **fossil fuels** at an increasing rate. We have burned coal, gas and oil to provide energy. Unfortunately, as well as providing energy, these fossil fuels have produced massive amounts of pollution known as **greenhouse gases**. These gases have had the serious effect of raising temperatures throughout the world, particularly over the last 50 years.

The main greenhouse gas is carbon dioxide (CO_2). This is how it contributes to global warming:

1 When fossil fuels are burned they release vast amounts of CO_2 into the atmosphere

2 These high levels of CO_2 absorb heat from the Earth's surface and so less heat escapes from the atmosphere

3 This means the temperature rises and the Earth becomes warmer.

The whole planet is affected by global warming, yet most of the CO_2 emissions come from a small number of developed and developing countries. For example, the United States of America produces over 25% of the world's CO_2 even though it has only 5% of the world's population! China is producing huge quantities of CO_2 and this trend looks set to increase. The results of global warming can already be seen. It is estimated that world temperatures will rise by between 1 and 6 degrees centigrade in the next 20 years if we keep on producing CO_2 at the current rate. If this happens, we may see the following devastating results:

→ Large areas of the world suffering from drought and famine

→ Sea levels rising and low-lying areas becoming flooded as a result of polar ice caps melting

→ The Gulf Stream may cool down or even stop altogether, bringing much colder weather in Ireland

→ Massive increase in floods, hurricanes, tornadoes and monsoons.

It is thought that climate change may cause water shortages in large areas of eastern Ireland, while low-lying areas, such as Cork City, could suffer from large-scale flooding.

To learn more about the issue of climate change, watch the movie 'An Inconvenient Truth' by former USA Vice-President Al Gore.

The Kyoto Protocol – a Solution?

The citizens of planet Earth are responsible for climate change and it is up to **all of us** to help reduce the problem. If we do not, it will become very difficult for future generations to live in certain parts of the world.

One way in which we may be able to have an impact on climate change is to reduce the amount of greenhouse gases we release into the environment. In December 1997, an international conference was held in Kyoto, Japan, and almost all the countries represented at the conference agreed to reduce the quanitity of greenhouse gases they were pumping into the atmosphere. They agreed to do this by:

- Reducing the amount of fossil fuels being burned
- Reducing the number of trees being cut down in poorer countries – this will help absorb greenhouse gases from the air
- Promoting the use of clean fuels as an alternative to fossil fuels.

Ireland has one of the worst records in the EU for greenhouse gas pollution. The government had hoped to reduce the amount Ireland is producing to just 13% higher than 1990 levels by the year 2012, by taking the measures outlined above. However, we are unlikey to meet this target, and by 2009, in fact, we had managed to increase dramatically the amount of greenhouse gases being released into the atmosphere. Ireland is the fifth worst polluter in the world! We need to change this and it is up to all of us to play our part.

Very few countries made any reductions in greenhouse gas production before February 2005, and to make matters worse, some of the worst offenders in the world are still increasing their emissions.

The Bali Agreement

In December 2007, another conference on climate change took place in Bali – an island in Indonesia. Most of the world's countries were represented at the conference. The result of the conference was an agreement called the **Bali Roadmap**.

The participating countries decided that climate change could only be tackled by **working together** to reduce the amount of greenhouse gases being released. The main agreement to come from the meeting was to promote the use of clean and alternative types of energy.

Questions

1 Explain the term 'climate change'.
2 What is CO_2?
3 Where do most greenhouse gas emissions come from?
4 What was the Kyoto Protocol? What were its aims?
5 What is the Bali Roadmap?
6 Can you list some alternative clean sources of energy that could be used in Ireland?

Green Energy

→ **Wind energy**

→ **Hydroelectric energy**

→ **Biomass**

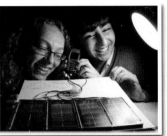

→ **Solar energy**

WALKING DEBATE
Green energy is always going to be the best type of energy for Ireland.

UN General Assembly Summit on Climate Change 2009

The United Nations General Assembly met on 22nd September 2009 to stress the importance of acting quickly on the problem of climate change. Some of the most powerful people in the world attended, such as the presidents of China, Japan and the United States of America. The following is an extract from the speech given by Ban Ki Moon, the Secretary General of the United Nations.

Excellencies, I am honoured to welcome you to this Summit – the largest-ever gathering of world leaders on climate change. Your presence bears witness to the gravity of the climate challenge. It is testament to the opportunity Copenhagen offers.

Your decisions will have momentous consequences. You have the power to chart a safer, more sustainable and prosperous course for this and future generations. The power to reduce the emissions that are causing climate change … to help the most vulnerable adapt to changes that are already under way … to catalyze a new era of global green growth.

Now is your moment to act.

Excellencies, greenhouse gas emissions continue to rise. We will soon reach critical thresholds. Consequences that we cannot reverse. The world's leading scientists warn that we have less than ten years to avoid the worst-case scenarios projected by the Intergovernmental Panel on Climate Change [IPCC].

Indeed those worst-case scenarios are becoming ever more likely. We must halt the rise in global emissions.

Earlier this month I was in the Arctic. I was alarmed by the rapid pace of change. The Arctic could be nearly ice-free by 2030. The consequences will be felt by people on every continent.

Just yesterday I met with many leaders from small island states. They were forceful and eloquent how climate change is rewriting their future.

All across Africa – the most vulnerable continent – climate change threatens to roll back years of development gains.

Climate change is the pre-eminent geopolitical and economic issue of the 21st century. It rewrites the global equation for development, peace and prosperity. It will increase pressure on water, food and land, reverse years of development gains, exacerbate poverty. destabilise fragile states and topple governments.

Some say tackling climate change is too expensive. They are wrong. The opposite is true. We will pay an unacceptable price if we do not act now.

(Source: www.un.org)

Pollution of International Waters

Oil is a very useful source of energy, at least for the time being. It is transported around the world's oceans every day in large oil tankers. Unfortunately, these tankers have accidents. There have been some disastrous oil spillages in our oceans as a result. Indeed, since 1979 it is estimated that over 1,000 million gallons of oil have ended up in the oceans.

Case Study

The *Prestige* Disaster

On 11th November 2002, the *Prestige*, a 26-year-old oil tanker carrying 77,000 tonnes of oil, was on its way from Latvia to Singapore when it ran into violent storms off the north-west coast of Spain. Two days later she began leaking oil into the sea and within hours birds, fish and sea plants were affected. Spain and Portugal would not allow the stricken tanker to be towed ashore to either country where it might have been possible to unload the oil.

Five days later, after all the crew members had been rescued, the *Prestige* was towed into international waters where waves were over 10 metres high. On 19th November she split in two and much of her load flowed into the north Atlantic. As well as destroying huge amounts of wildlife, plant life and fish, the effect on peoples' lives was immense. The Spanish province of Galicia was put on full alert. Over 150 kilometres of its coastline was contaminated by oil. It took months of work to clean the oil slick from the coastline and Galician fishermen lost large sums of money as they could not go back to the sea until the slick had been cleared. Tourism suffered in the area also as holiday-makers stayed away from the 90 beaches that had been affected.

The Spanish authorities were extremely angry that this disaster occurred and blamed the owners of the ship for allowing such an old vessel to carry a dangerous cargo so close to its coastline. The *Prestige* now lies at the bottom of the sea (along with over 300 other ships which have sunk along this stretch of the coast – which Galicians call the 'Coast of Death' – over the past century).

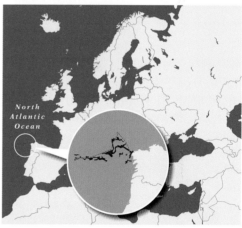

Extent of the oil spill off the Galician coast

Group Activity

Divide the class into the following groups:
1 The ship owners
2 The Spanish government
3 The local fishermen
4 Friends of the Earth environmental group
5 The crew of the *Prestige*.
   Each group should prepare a statement for a forthcoming television documentary entitled 'The *Prestige* Disaster – Who's to Blame?'
   A member from each group is then asked to make this statement on behalf of the group.

Student Task

Imagine that you are an official in the EU with responsibility for protecting EU waters. Draw up a list of things that you would do to make sure that large-scale environmental disasters do not happen in the future.

International Radioactive Pollution

Many countries throughout the world now generate energy by nuclear power, using small amounts of uranium. Some experts argue that nuclear power is a solution to climate change. In general it is seen as a clean way of creating energy, but unfortunately when things go wrong it may release radioactive materials into the world's environment. This material is dangerous to all living things on the planet. The waste created by the industry can also be hazardous. However, the most worrying thing is the possibility of accidents or leakages happening at the plants.

Chernobyl

The world's worst nuclear power plant disaster happened at Chernobyl in the Ukraine on 26th April 1986. An explosion at the plant caused 190 tonnes of radioactive material to be released into the atmosphere. The wind and rain clouds then transported the radioactive material throughout Europe, even as far as Ireland.

However, the areas near to Chernobyl suffered worst. Most of the nuclear fall-out affected neighbouring Belarus and its population of around 8 million people. Parts of Belarus have the most radioactive environment in the world. Large areas of land and towns have been evacuated. Much of the land still cannot be used to grow food or rear animals as it is too much of a health risk. It is thought that radioactive pollution has increased the levels of cancer cases here and that this may continue for generations to come.

CAMERAPRESS

CLASS DEBATE

Organise a class debate on the following topic: The Sellafield nuclear reprocessing plant in north-west England poses a threat to Ireland and should be closed down.

Read the poem by K. E. Boulding and answer the questions that follow:

The world is finite, resources are scarce,
Things are bad and will be worse,
Coal is burned and gas exploded,
Forests cut and soil eroded,
Wells are dry and air polluted,
Dust is blowing, trees are uprooted,
Oil is going, ores depleted,
Drains receive what is excreted,
Land is sinking, seas are rising,
Man is far too enterprising,
Fires will rage with man to fan it,
Soon we will have a plundered planet.

Questions

1 What is the poet telling us in the first two lines of the poem?
2 'Wells are dry and air polluted'. Why is this, in your opinion?
3 What is the reason for 'Land is sinking, seas are rising'?
4 Who does the poet blame for our 'plundered planet'?
5 Can you think of an appropriate title for this poem?
6 Write your own poem on the concept of stewardship.

Copenhagen Summit 2009

Most of the world's developed countries agree that climate change is one of the greatest challenges we face and that action must be taken to keep temperature increases below 2° centigrade.

Unfortunately, at the Copenhagen Summit in 2009, not all countries would sign an agreement to make this happen. Some poorer countries were unwilling to commit to the agreement.

Questions

1 Can you suggest some reasons why these poorer countries would not sign the agreement.
2 Find out which organisation arranged the Copenhagen Summit.
3 Do summits such as the one in Copenhagen help improve our environment? Explain your answer.

Ideas For Taking Action

4.4

Organise an information/awareness day for your school on the topic: 'Nuclear Power – Lessons from the Chernobyl Disaster'.

SKILLS YOU MIGHT USE:
→ Information gathering
→ Information processing
→ Poster design
→ Communication with agencies
→ Planning
→ Issuing invitations

Can you think of other skills you may need to undertake this action?

Stewardship – Sample Examination Questions

1 (i)   The amount of greenhouse gases produced by a person each year is called a C _____
N _____

(ii)   The process of burning waste under controlled conditions is called I _____

(iii)   A political party that places a great emphasis on stewardship and the environment is the
G _____ P _____

(iv)   Climate change may cause low-lying areas in Ireland to suffer from large-scale F _____

(v)   B _____ is the burning of natural materials such as wood to provide energy

(vi)   An example of a Green Energy in plentiful supply in Ireland is W _____

(vii)   The B _____ R _____ is an agreement to promote the use of clean and
alternative types of energy

(viii)   The world's worst nuclear disaster happened in C _____

2   A number of families, including your family, have been affected by severe flooding in your local area.
The families have now decided to set up an action committee to look for help. You have been chosen
as a representative on this committee.

(i)   Name an organisation that the committee could ask for help and give at least two reasons why
you have chosen this organisation

(ii)   Write a letter to your local newspaper explaining what the action committee is trying to achieve.
You should try and mention at least two things the committee is trying to achieve

(iii)   Describe two ways in which your school could become active in helping your committee

Website Watch
Check out the following websites for further information on the concept of Stewardship:

www.change.ie
www.sei.ie
www.foei.org
www.friendsoftheirishenvironment.net
www.carbonfootprint.com
www.climatechange.com
www.epa.ie

www.stopclimatechaos.ie
www.cultivate.ie
www.oxfam.org
www.ipcc.ch
www.un.org/wcm/content/site/climatechange/gateway
www.enfo.ie

TAKING ACTION

Organise the planting of trees and shrubs in the grounds of your school

This is a very practical way to take action and make a real difference to the environment. The concept of stewardship focuses on looking after and trying to improve the environment. By planting trees and shrubs, you are making the school surroundings more attractive and also you will be helping to clear the atmosphere of greenhouse gases.

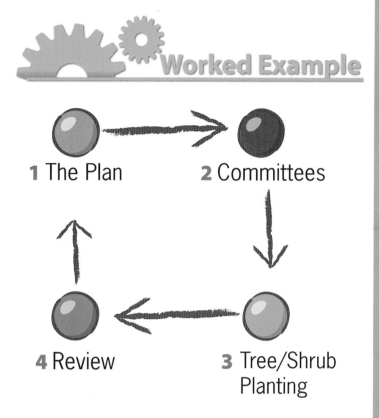

Worked Example

1 The Plan → **2** Committees → **3** Tree/Shrub Planting → **4** Review →

The plan:

What do we need to find out?
What preparation needs to be done?
Who do we need to help us?
When do we want to do this?

Committees:

What committees do we need to make the action work?
How do we assign students to committees?
What is the responsibility of each committee?

PREPARATION COMMITTEE — PERMISSION COMMITTEE — FINANCE COMMITTEE

PUBLICITY COMMITTEE — WELCOMING COMMITTEE — PLANTING COMMITTEE — THANK YOU COMMITTEE

The above is a list of committees that may be needed – can you think of any others?

Tree and shrub planting ceremony:

The main point of this action is to plant trees and shrubs somewhere in the school grounds. It is essential to get permission from the school authorities to do this. You may decide to buy some trees and shrubs from a local nursery or, if you're lucky, the nursery may be willing to sponsor the plants. Try and plant trees and shrubs that are native to Ireland. You may also like to invite some special guests to help with the planting ceremony e.g. a local politician or environmental activist. Why not also invite the local media to record the event?

The review:

The review will help you analyse and find out how successful the projects were. You will need to see the positive and negative results of your work. It is also very important to note the various skills that all members of the class used when undertaking the action.

Write down at least five new things that you have learned while undertaking the action.

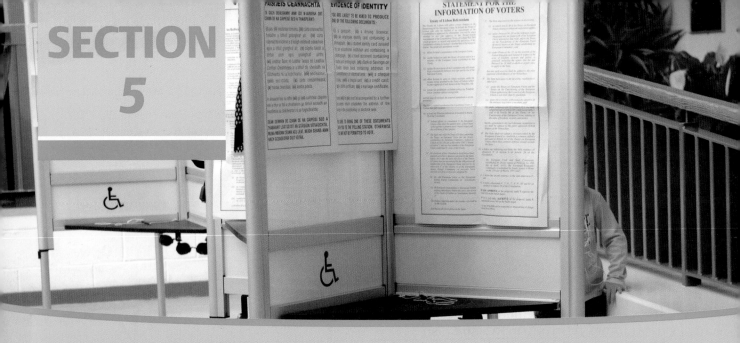

Democracy

In this section we will explore the workings of democracy at individual, local, national and international levels. We will also look at how you, the citizen, have an important role to play in the workings of democracy.

What is Democracy?

Democracy is a form of government and it is the way we run our country in Ireland. The word democracy comes from two Greek words; *Demos* which means 'people' and *Kratia* which means 'to rule'. Put simply democracy means 'rule by the people'. Power is in the hands of the people because it is they who elect others to run the country on their behalf. Abraham Lincoln described democracy as

> **'Government of the people, by the people, for the people'.**

The birth of democracy can be traced back to ancient Greece. Athens, a state in Greece at that time, was ruled by a **direct democracy**. This meant that the citizens had a direct say in how the state was run. This was possible because the population of Athens was quite small then. All the citizens met in an assembly and made their views known. However, to be considered a citizen of Athens, you had to be male and own property, and you had to have been born in Athens. Women, slaves and people not born in Athens were not considered to be citizens and so had no say in the running of the state.

The democracy we live under today is called a **representative democracy**. Because the population of the Irish Republic is around 4 million, it would be impossible for all its citizens to have a direct say in affairs of state, so we elect representatives to run things on our behalf. The citizens of a democracy hold elections to choose their representatives. Every citizen over the age of 18 can vote in these elections for the candidate of their choice.

What Does Democracy Mean To Me?

Because you, the citizen, live in a democratic state, you have certain rights and freedoms:

- The **right to** be treated **equally**, regardless of gender, colour, race, religion or social standing

- **Freedom of expression**. This entitles you to express your opinion and to partake in debates. Individuals are also entitled to express their opinions through the media by means of television, newspapers and radio. This is also called the free press

- The **right to criticise** the government if you do not agree with its policies or laws. You may do this by organising or participating in a protest, signing a petition, or lobbying the government on an issue you feel strongly about

- The **right** to **vote** in elections

- The **right** to **run for election**

- The **right** to **equality** before the law

- Freedom to **practice your religion**

- Freedom to set up or **join associations**, **organisations**, **political parties** or **trade unions**.

Democracy is also based on the principle of **majority rule** and **minority rights**. This means that decisions are made on the basis of majority agreement, but the rights and freedoms of those in the minority must be respected. The voice of the minority is listened to. In addition, democracies generally have a number of political parties, each with its own differing views on how the country should be run.

Not all countries are democracies. Some countries in the world are under **authoritarian rule**. Under this form of rulership, citizens don't possess the freedoms or rights that we have under democratic rule. For example, the government may ban opposing political parties. Sometimes citizens are banned from joining various organisations or associations and their right to express their opinion is violated. Protesters and those who openly criticise the government are imprisoned and those who belong to minority religions can be persecuted. Examples of authoritarian rule include dictatorships, countries under military rule or countries under communist rule. Examples include China, North Korea, Sudan, Cuba and Myanmar (Burma).

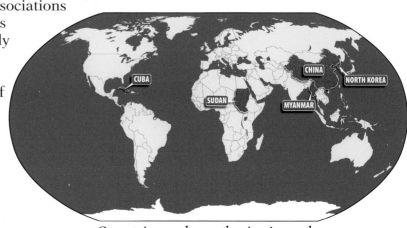

Countries under authoritarian rule

Some Thoughts on Democracy

If liberty and equality, as is thought by some, are chiefly to be found in democracy, they will be best attained when all persons alike share in the government to the utmost.
Aristotle, 384–322 BC, Greek philosopher

A great democracy must be progressive or it will soon cease to be a great democracy.

Theodore Roosevelt, 1858–1919, American President

The true democrat is he who with purely non-violent means defends his liberty and therefore, his country's and ultimately that of the whole of mankind.
Mahatma Gandhi, 1869–1948, philosopher and peace activist

The motivating force of the theory of a democratic way of life is still a belief that as individuals we live cooperatively, and, to the best of our ability, serve the community in which we live, and that our own success, to be real, must contribute to it.

Eleanor Roosevelt, 1884–1962, human rights activist

CAMERAPRESS 2, ALAMY 1, SHUTTERSTOCK 1

Talking Point

1 What is meant by 'democracy'?
2 Where did democracy originate?
3 Outline the differences between democracy in Ancient Greece and the democracy you live under today.
4 What are the main differences between direct democracies and representative democracies?
5 What is authoritarian rule?
6 Under a democracy what rights is an individual entitled to?
7 What are the differences between democratic countries and countries under authoritarian rule.
8 Reread the quotes about democracy. Whose did you like the best and why?

Wordsearch on Democracy

Complete the following wordsearch

E	X	O	U	S	Q	M	E	M	C	F	R	B	D	Z	A	P	G	E	D
B	A	N	B	G	V	L	R	J	X	J	X	Y	N	R	N	P	O	Y	I
K	R	U	U	E	R	P	N	G	A	R	T	K	K	H	W	U	V	T	R
L	R	E	T	I	K	A	X	C	G	Z	T	J	B	W	L	U	E	I	E
Y	O	J	G	H	E	B	Q	R	C	A	X	N	O	X	U	T	R	R	C
O	T	H	A	G	O	D	L	T	J	H	U	N	U	A	S	I	N	O	T
F	T	I	R	E	P	R	E	S	E	N	T	A	T	I	V	E	M	N	Q
S	R	W	R	I	I	M	I	D	U	S	G	T	W	E	W	Y	E	I	Q
F	F	E	W	O	X	F	E	T	N	S	U	E	S	S	Y	O	N	M	A
K	Z	L	E	Z	J	M	F	E	A	F	B	A	Q	L	K	B	T	M	E
S	U	N	N	D	O	A	Z	O	C	R	S	N	O	I	T	C	E	L	E
M	J	W	R	C	O	I	M	P	O	L	I	T	I	C	S	L	S	S	X
Q	R	I	R	R	T	M	T	J	J	O	G	A	M	K	L	Y	P	S	A
A	G	A	H	I	W	B	T	C	O	N	W	R	N	I	G	Z	R	L	N
J	C	E	C	M	D	S	S	G	T	D	Y	O	P	B	G	N	F	S	Y
Y	X	W	M	K	C	S	B	R	P	M	F	E	T	L	G	Q	T	L	Q
P	R	J	T	S	E	U	A	O	Y	U	E	S	W	F	X	Z	A	X	O
Z	I	M	M	R	F	D	Z	T	J	X	H	N	G	V	B	T	H	W	Q
D	T	O	J	Q	Q	J	C	J	U	W	B	N	N	M	Z	T	F	L	H
M	G	U	V	A	I	Y	R	B	T	C	C	P	I	I	Y	S	C	P	H

- ■ AUTHORITARIAN
- ■ CITIZENS
- ■ DEMOCRACY
- ■ DIRECT
- ■ ELECTIONS
- ■ FREEDOM
- ■ GOVERNMENT
- ■ MAJORITY
- ■ MINORITY
- ■ POLITICS
- ■ REPRESENTATIVE
- ■ RIGHTS

Ideas For Taking Action

5.1

1. Organise 'Democracy Day' in your school to raise awareness of what it is to live in a democracy. The day could consist of a poster display or exhibition outlining the history of democracy from Ancient Greece to the present time.

SKILLS YOU MIGHT USE:
- → Planning
- → Research
- → Internet
- → Artistic/design
- → Communication

Can you think of other skills you may need to undertake this action?

CHAPTER 5.2

Our Democratic Community

Democracy in action is evident in the many communities you belong to, from the school community to the wider community. A democratic community is one in which all members are given the right to **participate**, **make decisions** or **elect people** to act on their behalf.

Our Democratic School – the Work of the Student Council

Virtually all school communities have a **student council** in place. A student council provides a forum whereby the views of students are expressed and taken on board by teachers and school management. Like other democratic institutions, students are elected to the council to represent their schoolmates and make decisions on their behalf. The extract below outlines what is involved in a student council:

Hi! My name is Conor Dunphy and I am a fifth-year student in St Luke's Community School. The student council was set up in my school in 1994 and has been running ever since. The council is made up of two students from each year. The council elects one of its members to act as chairperson and another member to act as secretary. The secretary records the minutes (what everyone says) of every meeting. We also have a 'link teacher' who brings any issues raised at the council meetings to the attention of the school principal and staff.

The council meets once a month and provides a platform where student representatives raise important issues on behalf of their fellow students.

I didn't get involved with the student council until third year. It was only then that I realised that the best way of making a difference was to become an active member of the Student Council. With this in mind I decided to run for election.

Every class in every year can nominate a candidate. Every January, a school council election takes place and two students from each year are elected to the council. Council election time is quite exciting because the candidates get a chance to campaign. Then students can vote for the people they want to represent them in the council. As a council we have raised a number of issues and made decisions on behalf of the student

population. Over the last couple of years a number of changes have taken place, thanks to the work of the student council. For example, the council felt that senior students should wear different colour jumpers from junior students. This issue was raised at a council meeting and was voted on. An overwhelming majority voted in favour of this proposal. As a result a new 'senior' jumper was introduced.

The school council, in my opinion, is a great example of a democratic community. It enables the student voice to be heard and I feel that this voice is listened to and taken seriously by both teachers and students. I would highly recommend any student to get involved with their student council.

Questions

1 In what ways can the student council be considered a democratic community?
2 List the members of the school council.
3 What democratic decisions have been made by St Luke's student council?

What is a Student Council?

A Student Council is a representative structure for students only, through which they can become involved in the affairs of the school, working in partnership with school management, staff and parents for the benefit of the school and its students.

Does your school have the right to set up a student council?

The Education Act 1998 states that Boards of Management must encourage and give all reasonable assistance to students in the formation and running of student councils. The National Children's Strategy states that children and young people will have a voice in matters that affect their lives and be provided with opportunities to participate in decision making.

Democracy in the Wider Community

There are many democratic organisations at work in the wider community. Let's look at some of them. Examples are:

- Credit Unions
- GAA and Sports Clubs
- Residents Associations
- Youth clubs
- Scout and Guide Associations.

Can you think of any other organisations in your community that could be considered democratic?

Comhairle na nÓg

Comhairle na nÓg are local youth councils which afford young people the opportunity to become involved in, and have their say on, issues that affect them at local level and national level. There is a Comhairle na nÓg in each city and county. Some members of this organisation are elected to **Dáil na nÓg** which is an annual national parliament for 12-18 year olds. Find out more about the work of Comhairle na nÓg on www.comhairlenanog.ie.

Ideas For Taking Action 5.2

1. Organise and run the student council elections in your school.

SKILLS YOU MIGHT USE:
→ Planning
→ Organising
→ Public relations
→ Communication
→ Leadership
→ Mathematical
→ Computer skills
→ Design skills

Can you think of other skills you may need to undertake this action?

2. Invite a guest speaker from Dáil na nÓg or another democratically-run organisation in your community to your class. Find out about the workings of democracy in that organisation.

→ Planning
→ Letter-writing
→ Telephone
→ Communication
→ Hosting
→ Questioning
→ Listening
→ Reporting

Can you think of other skills you may need to undertake this action?

Ireland: A Democratic State

The basic laws of the Irish state are laid down in a document known as the **Constitution**. Ireland's constitution is called **Bunreacht na hÉireann**. It was written and adopted by the Irish people in 1937. Bunreacht na hÉireann outlines how Ireland is governed, the key laws of the state, the roles and powers of key political figures and the rights we are entitled to as Irish citizens.

The constitution is divided into sections called **articles**. The main articles are described below:

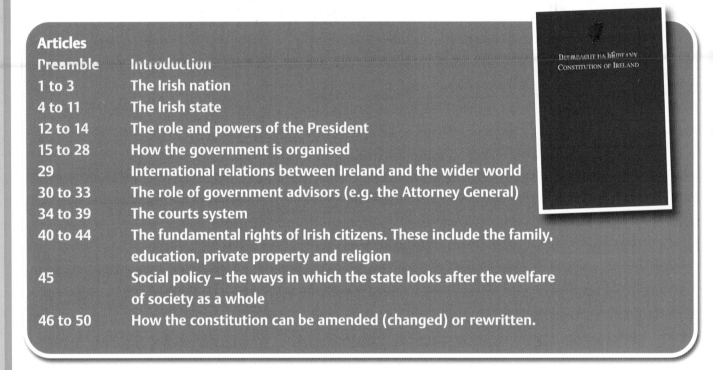

Articles	
Preamble	Introduction
1 to 3	The Irish nation
4 to 11	The Irish state
12 to 14	The role and powers of the President
15 to 28	How the government is organised
29	International relations between Ireland and the wider world
30 to 33	The role of government advisors (e.g. the Attorney General)
34 to 39	The courts system
40 to 44	The fundamental rights of Irish citizens. These include the family, education, private property and religion
45	Social policy – the ways in which the state looks after the welfare of society as a whole
46 to 50	How the constitution can be amended (changed) or rewritten.

Our society is in a constant state of change. As a result of this, laws also have to change and this in turn may involve amending or changing the constitution. However, we cannot alter our constitution unless the majority of people in Ireland agree to do so. The people can decide by voting in a **referendum**, a special election whereby they vote either **Yes** or **No** to a proposed change.

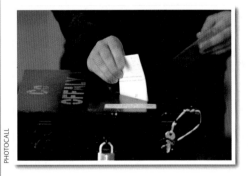

The Irish constitution has been changed numerous times. Some of Ireland's more recent referendums include:

■ The Nice Treaty (1992) – this reformed the institutional structure of the European Union
■ The Divorce Referendum (1995) – this lifted the ban on divorce introduced by Éamon de Valera in 1937
■ The Lisbon Treaty (2007 and 2009) – this amended previous treaties on the European Union.

How Ireland is Governed

The **Oireachtas** is the name given to Ireland's national parliament. The Oireachtas consists of:

1 The **President**
2 The House of Representatives called **Dáil Éireann**
3 The Senate or the **Seanad**.

The main function of the Oireachtas is to govern the country and make laws on behalf of its citizens.

This diagram shows how Ireland is governed.

Leinster House – The seat of Dáil and Seanad Éireann

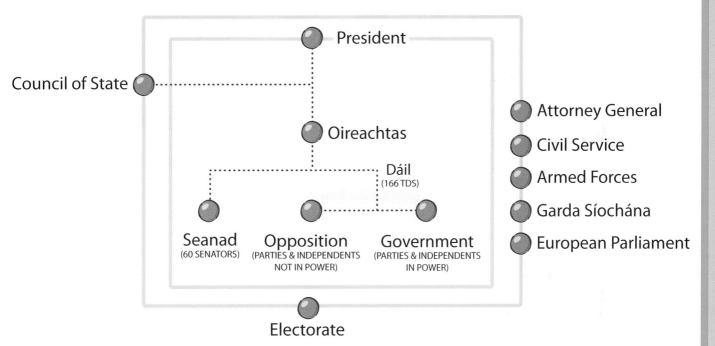

The Role of the President

Áras an Uachtaráin

The **Irish President** (Uachtaráin na hÉireann) is Ireland's Head of State. He or she is elected by the people and is elected for a term of seven years. The President's official residence is **Áras an Uachtaráin**, situated in Phoenix Park in Dublin. Bunreacht na hÉireann outlines the role and powers of the President. These include:

- Safeguarding our constitution
- Signing bills so that they become law
- Ensuring that new laws do not infringe on the rights of Irish citizens
- Representing Ireland abroad
- Being the Commander-in-Chief of our defence forces
- Giving new ministers their seal of office.

Ireland's Presidents

Douglas Hyde
Elected 1938

Seán T. Ó Ceallaigh
Elected 1945

Éamon de Valera
Elected 1959

Erskine Childers
Elected 1973

Cearbhall Ó Dálaigh
Elected 1974

Patrick Hillery
Elected 1976

Mary Robinson
Elected 1990

Mary McAleese
Elected 1997

Written Work

1 In what year was the Irish constitution written?
2 How many articles does the constitution contain?
3 What is a referendum?
4 What is meant by an **amendment to** the constitution?
5 What is the Oireachtas? Who or what makes up the Oireachtas?
6 Outline the main role and powers of Uachtarán na hÉireann
7 What president held office when you were born?
8 Who is the current president?

The Houses of the Oireachtas

The Irish parliament (the Oireachtas) is made up of two houses.
1 The **Dáil**
2 The **Seanad**.
Their main role is to make new laws and to govern the country on our behalf. Let's have a look at these two houses in more detail.

The Dáil

The Dáil sits in **Leinster House** in Dublin. It is made up of **166** elected representatives called **TDs (Teachta Dála)**. They are elected to the Dáil by Irish citizens. For election purposes, Ireland is divided into **43** areas – these are called **constituencies**. The people who live in these constituencies elect either three, four or five TDs depending on the amount of people living in that constituency.

Map of Ireland's Constituencies

The main functions of the Dáil are as follows:
- To make or pass new laws
- To advise the government on the social, economic and financial life of the country
- To debate issues of the day
- To make decisions on behalf of Irish citizens.

Dáil proceedings are chaired by the **Ceann Comhairle**. He or she ensures that order is maintained during Dáil debates. The Ceann Comhairle is an elected TD.

The interior of the Dáil

The Role of the TD (Teachta Dála)

TDs play a very important role in the Dáil. They represent the interests of people living in their constituencies. In addition they can make and pass new laws. Some TDs are members of committees that review proposed laws or investigate issues of national importance.

TDs do not spend all their time in the Dáil, however. It is important that they meet with their constituents on a regular basis. Many TDs hold clinics where they advise constituents on a wide range of issues. To get a deeper insight into the work of a TD, read the interview below.

An Interview with Joan Burton, TD

What constituency do you represent?
I am a Dáil Deputy for the Dublin West constituency, which is a rapidly growing constituency that covers areas as diverse in their social make-up as Castleknock and Mulhuddart and includes the Connolly Hospital, the Blanchardstown Shopping Centre and Dublin airport within its boundaries.

When were you elected?
I was first elected to the Dáil in 1992 and again in 2002 and in 2007.

What does your job involve?
I am a TD for the Labour Party. I am also the Deputy Leader of the Labour Party and that party's spokesperson on Finance which makes me a key player in challenging the government's economic and financial policies in such critical areas as unemployment, credit and the prosperity of our country.

I attend the Dáil on Tuesdays, Wednesdays and Thursdays when it is sitting. I deal with phone calls and correspondence from constituents and interest groups. My role as a TD is legislative which means I can propose and amend legislation which forms the law of the land.

I also meet my constituents on a regular basis and deal with issues they raise. I attend numerous public meetings about matters concerning my constituency.

Do you like your job?
I love my job as a TD. I particularly enjoy speaking in the Dáil, fighting for a fair and just Ireland as well as meeting people and helping them where possible.

The Seanad

Seanad Éireann is the name given to Ireland's senate. Members of the senate are called **senators**. The Seanad is less powerful than the Dáil. Its main role is to consider and review bills (proposed laws) that the government wants passed. The Seanad also has the power to propose new laws. There are **60** senators elected to the Seanad, but not everyone can vote in senate elections.

- 6 senators are elected by universities. Only university graduates may vote in these elections
- 11 are nominated by the Taoiseach
- the remaining 43 are elected from five panels, each panel representing particular interests in Irish society, namely:

1 Administration
2 Agriculture
3 Culture and education
4 Industry and commerce
5 Labour and work.

The interior of Seanad Éireann

MICHAEL QUINN

FIND OUT

1. The names of three current senators.
2. The current leader of Seanad Éireann.

Talking Point

1 Name the two Houses of the Oireachtas.
2 What are constituencies? How many are there in Ireland?
3 Describe the functions of a TD.
4 What is the role of the Ceann Comhairle?
5 What is the main role of the Seanad?
6 Find out the following:
 - The name of the constituency in which you live
 - The number of TDs who represent your constituency
 - The names of your local TDs.

The Government

The basic role of the government is to run the affairs of the state. The government is usually decided by a **general election**. The political party that receives the most votes forms the government. If one party does not receive a majority (51% of seats in the Dáil), it may invite other parties to join with it to form the government. This is called a **coalition government**.

The main functions of the government involve:

- Making new laws
- Managing the financial affairs of the state
- Managing the economy
- Managing the social affairs of the Irish people
- Overseeing the provision and improvement of essential services
- Planning for the future
- Forging links with other countries.

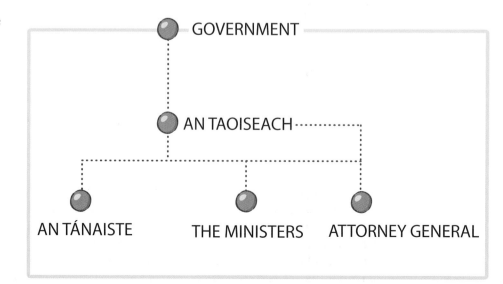

GOVERNMENT

AN TAOISEACH

AN TÁNAISTE   THE MINISTERS   ATTORNEY GENERAL

The Cabinet

The Taoiseach, the Tánaiste and principal government ministers are often referred to as **the cabinet**. It is made up of at least seven and no more than fifteen members. Each member of the cabinet is responsible for a particular government department. Cabinet meetings take place on a regular basis and makes decisions that affect the lives of the Irish people. Members of the cabinet must speak with one voice and must stand together on all policy matters. This is called **collective responsibility**.

FIND OUT

1. The party or parties which make up the current government.
2. The name of the current Taoiseach and his/her political party.
3. The name of the current Tánaiste and his/her political party.

The Taoiseach

The Taoiseach is the Prime Minister of the Irish state. He or she is the leader of the government and is elected by the Dáil after a general election. The Taoiseach is normally the leader of the party who has the most seats in the Dáil.

The Taoiseach has many responsibilities. He or she:

- Provides leadership
- Controls government business
- Appoints (and dismisses) cabinet ministers
- Chairs cabinet meetings
- Nominates senators
- Decides when a general election will take place
- Meets with world leaders
- Defends government decisions.

The Tánaiste

The Tánaiste is the deputy Prime Minister. He or she holds a cabinet post and also acts as head of government when the Taoiseach is out of the country.

The Ministers

The Taoiseach cannot run the country alone. He or she therefore assembles a team that assist in the task. Members of this team are called ministers and each minister is responsible for the running of a particular government department. These departments look after the social, economic, political and cultural affairs of the state. The most important government departments are:

■ The Department of Finance

This department is responsible for the financial affairs of the country. The Minister for Finance decides how much money must be raised each year in taxes and how much money each government department is to be given. He or she must also prepare a budget which states how much the country will receive and allocate that year.

■ The Department of Social and Family Affairs

This department looks after the social welfare needs of various sectors of society, notably parents, the elderly, the disabled and the unemployed. This department also provides essential services and support to various members of society.

■ The Department of Health and Children

This department is responsible for the provision of our health service. It manages health boards that provide communities with hospitals and medical staff, and also provides information and support to those who need it. In addition, this department promotes healthy living and leads many campaigns such as anti-drug and anti-smoking campaigns. This department also pays particular attention to the needs of children.

■ The Department of Education and Science

This department looks after primary, post-primary and third level education in Ireland. It ensures that the educational needs of Irish citizens are met. It provides schools with funds and grants, and pays teachers' salaries.

■ The Department of Justice, Equality and Law Reform

The main function of this department is to uphold and enforce the laws of the state. This department is responsible for the Gardaí, prison service and courts service. It also safeguards the rights and freedoms of Irish citizens.

FIND OUT

Other key government departments are listed in the table below. Find out the responsibilities of each one and also the name of the current minister in charge of it.

GOVERNMENT DEPARTMENT	RESPONSIBILITY	NAME OF CURRENT MINISTER
An Taoiseach		
Agriculture, Fisheries and Food		
Arts, Sport and Tourism		
Environment, Heritage and Local Government		
Transport		
Enterprise, Trade and Employment		
Defence		
Community, Rural and Gaeltacht Affairs		
Communications, Energy and Natural Resources		
Foreign Affairs		

The Attorney General

The Attorney General is appointed by the Taoiseach, is a member of the cabinet and acts as the chief legal advisor to the government. The Attorney General is usually consulted when the government is preparing new laws. He or she may also represent the government in legal proceedings.

FIND OUT

Who is the current Attorney General?

The Civil Service

The civil service is often referred to as the 'administrative arm' of the government. Civil service is the collective term for the permanent staff of the departments of state and some state agencies. Its main role is to advise the government on policy and carry out the day-to-day running of government departments. Civil servants must also carry out decisions made by governments.

Questions
1 Who makes up the cabinet?
2 What are ministers? What do they do?
3 What is the role of the Attorney General?
4 What is the civil service?

Influencing the Government

Because you live in a democracy, you as a citizen have the power to influence the government on issues you feel strongly about. There are different ways to do this:

1 Join an **interest group**. These groups protect the interests of members and campaign on their behalf. Examples of interest groups include trade unions and the Irish Farmers Association.

2 Get involved in a **pressure group**. Pressure groups are so-called because they put pressure on the government to support their cause. Greenpeace and Amnesty International are examples.

Both interest and pressure groups, and others, use various means of influencing the government. These include:

■ **Petitions:** Individuals or groups may wish to bring an issue they feel strongly about to the attention of the government and a petition is a good way of doing so. It involves the collection of signatures from people who are concerned about that issue. Petitions are usually presented to members of the government.

■ **Lobbying:** Lobbying involves putting pressure on the government by means of letter-writing campaigns, meeting with members of the government and by getting media attention.

PHOTOCALL 3

■ **Protest** and **protest marches**

■ **Strikes**

IMAGINE!

Imagine the government made a law that reduced school holidays to just three weeks a year. You are unhappy with this new law. What could you do to influence the government to change this law?

Political Parties

Political parties are the 'hub' of democracy in Ireland. Each party has a particular idea about how the country should be run. Political parties nominate a candidate to run in the various elections that take place.

There are a number of political parties in Ireland. The main ones are:

■ **Fianna Fáil**
■ **Fine Gael**
■ **Labour**
■ **Sinn Féin**
■ **Green Party**

There are several smaller political parties too.

Not all politicians belong to a political party. Some are **independent**, which means they do not belong to a party but stand for a particular cause or represent local or regional issues.

Group Activity

Divide the class into groups. Each group must research one of the political parties listed on the previous page. For each party each group must:

1 Name the leader.

2 Find out that party's views on how the country should be run (in terms of education, health, social welfare, employment, rights and responsibilities).

3 Name any TDs representing that party in the Dáil who are not in the cabinet. What do they do when not in the Dáil?

IMAGINE!

Imagine that you formed your own political party.
1. What would your party be called?
2. What would the logo of your party look like? Draw it.
3. What changes should be made? Outline five ideas in your CSPE notebook.

Local Government

Every household in Ireland is served by **local government** in the form of a **local authority**. Each authority is responsible for a particular locality and its main purpose is to provide essential services to the people who live in that locality. Ireland is divided into 114 local authorities.

Different types of local authorities operate in Ireland. These include:
- County councils
- City councils
- Borough councils
- Town councils.

The new Dublin bike scheme

Services Provided by Local Authorities

Local authorities provide a wide range of services within the area they serve, including:

1 Housing and building
2 Road transport and safety (including street lights)
3 Water supply and sewage
4 Recreation and amenities
5 Agriculture, education, health and welfare
6 Development incentives and controls
7 Environmental protection
8 Miscellaneous services.

Who is the Local Authority?

Local authorities are democratic in that the members are elected by the people who live within that authority. Local elections take place every five years. The people elected are called **councillors**. The main role of a councillor is to serve the needs of the local community.

Councillors are assisted in their work by a **County Manager** who oversees the day-to-day running of the local authority. Councillors usually meet once a month to discuss the business of the local authority. Unlike TDs, councillors are not paid a salary as their work is mainly voluntary. They do, however, receive annual expenses.

FIND OUT!

The names of local councillors in your area.

Questions

1 List the services provided by local authorities.
2 What are elected representatives to local authorities called?
3 Who oversees day-to-day running of the local authority?

Elections

Elections are the backbone of democracy. They are the means by which the people can choose or elect representatives to act on their behalf. An individual running for election is called a **candidate**.

Irish citizens may vote in the following elections:

1 **Local Elections** – these are held every five years to elect representatives to the local authority.
2 **By-Elections** – these elections take place when a Dáil seat becomes vacant. This usually happens when a TD either dies or resigns his or her seat.
3 **General Elections** – a general election usually takes place every five years. This election elects 166 TDs to the Dáil.
4 **Presidential Elections** – this election take place every seven years and elects the Irish President.
5 **European Elections** – European elections take place every five years and elect MEPs to the European Parliament.
6 **Referendums** – a special election which asks the people if some part of the constitution should be changed.

Elections take place in **polling stations**. These are usually in a local school or community centre.

It is vital that everybody votes in elections. Study this poster and answer the questions that follow.

Talking Point

1 What elections are this poster encouraging people to vote in?
2 What date must you register by?
3 Who is this poster aimed at? Explain your answer.
4 Name four places you can get a registration form from?
5 What organisation is responsible for this poster?

Voting

Voting is the means by which citizens are given the opportunity to choose public representatives or indicate their agreement or otherwise with a proposed change to the constitution.

Who Can Vote?

All Irish citizens can vote if they are **over 18** and their name is on the **electoral register**. The electoral register is simply a list of all Irish citizens eligible to vote. Citizens can find out if they're registered to vote by asking to see the register at their local library or post office.

In a democracy, every citizen that meets these requirements has the right to vote. However, not all citizens exercise this right, which many see as a responsibility.

> **Can you list some reasons why citizens choose not to vote in elections?**

The System of Voting in Ireland

The system of voting in Ireland is called **proportional representation**. It is called this because the number of seats a party wins is in proportion to the number of votes it receives. In other words, if a party gets 10% of the votes, it should get 10% of the seats. This system ensures that minority (smaller) parties or independent (non-party) candidates are represented in the Dáil.

Proportional representation enables the voter to indicate his or her first choice of candidate, second choice, third choice, and so on. The example below illustrates how this system works.

The voter has given Mary Murphy his first preference vote. If Mary Murphy is either elected with a surplus of votes over the quota (see below) or eliminated, her vote goes to the number two choice, Michael Wyatt. If Michael Wyatt is elected or eliminated, the vote then goes to the third preference Anthony Byrne. This is called the **Single Transferable Vote** (**STV**).

Candidate	Vote
John O'Reilly	5
Mary Murphy	1
Anthony Byrne	3
Patricia Nolan	6
Michael Wyatt	2
Geraldine Potter	4

How to Vote

Prior to an election or referendum, those eligible to vote receive a **polling card**. The voter's name and address are clearly marked on the card. On the day of an election the voter must produce this polling card along with proof of identity. This can be a passport, driving licence or student card, for example. **A polling clerk** will then put a mark against the voter's name on the electoral register. This enables the voter turnout to be calculated. The voter is then given a **ballot paper** on which the names of the candidates up for election are listed.

Voting is by **secret ballot**. This means that the voter indicates his or her preference in private. To ensure privacy, polling booths (cubicles) are set up in the polling stations. Voters indicate their preference by writing the number 1 beside their first preference, 2 beside their second preference, and so on.

Ballot paper

When the choices have been made, the ballot paper is then placed into a **ballot box**. When the polling station closes, ballot boxes are sealed and taken to a central counting place for the constituency.

Counting the Votes

The counting of votes is supervised by the **returning officer**. Before the count begins the **quota** is calculated. The quota is the number of votes a candidate needs to be elected. The formula below decides the quota for each constituency:

$$\text{Quota} = \frac{\text{Total valid poll}}{\text{number of seats} + 1} + 1$$

The **total valid poll** is calculated by counting the number of votes cast and subtracting invalid or spoiled votes. A **spoiled vote** is a ballot paper that has been incorrectly filled out, has been defaced in some way or has not been validated with an official stamp. For example, in a four-seat constituency the quota is calculated as follows:

Total Number of Votes Cast		45,000
Number of Spoiled Votes		- 450
Total Valid Poll		44,550
Quota	=	$\frac{44,550}{(4+1)}$ +1
	=	$\frac{44,550}{5}$
	divided by	
	=	8,910 +1
	=	8,911

In our example the quota is 8,911. A candidate needs 8,911 votes to be elected.

When the quota has been established, the votes are then sorted for each candidate and then counted. The people responsible for this are called **tellers**. The first count sorts out the amount of number 1 votes each candidate has. If a candidate reaches the quota, he or she is elected. If not, the candidate with the smallest number of votes is eliminated. Using the STV, the eliminated candidate's second preference votes are then redistributed among the other candidates. This process will continue until a candidate reaches the quota and is elected. If it is a multi-seat constituency, the surplus votes of those elected are transferred to those candidates who have not yet reached the quota.

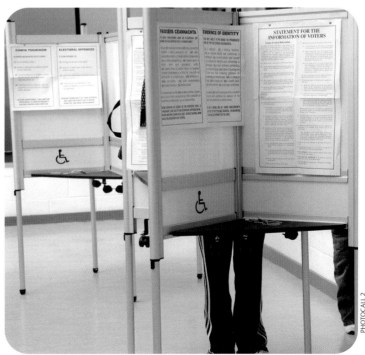

Written work

1. Make a list of elections in which an Irish citizen of voting age can vote.
2. What system of voting is used in Irish elections? How does it work?
3. What is a quota?
4. Calculate the quota for three polling stations. The information you require is set out below:

Polling Station One   **(3 seats)**
Total number of votes cast   60,000
Number of spoiled votes   400
Total valid poll   ?
Quota   ?

Polling Station Two   **(2 seats)**
Total number of votes cast   30,000
Number of spoiled votes   200
Total valid poll   ?
Quota   ?

Polling Station Three   **(4 seats)**
Total number of votes cast   100,000
Number of spoiled votes   600
Total valid poll   ?
Quota   ?

Secret Ballot

As a class choose three candidates (living or dead) for the title of 'Greatest Irish Citizen'. Using a secret ballot, write the name of the person you feel is most deserving of the title and place it in a box. Elect someone from the class to count the votes.

Northern Ireland

Northern Ireland consists of six counties – Antrim, Armagh, Derry, Down, Fermanagh and Tyrone. Northern Ireland has a number of political parties. The main political parties are:

- The Democratic Unionist Party (DUP)

- Sinn Féin

- The Social Democratic and Labour Party (SDLP)

- The Alliance Party of Northern Ireland

- The Ulster Unionist Party (UUP)

Stormont building

The political parties of Northern Ireland can be broadly divided into two types. **Nationalist** political parties believe in a united island of Ireland. **Unionist** parties, on the other hand, want to remain part of the United Kingdom. Over the decades there has been much conflict between those with Nationalist and Unionist beliefs. Some people have turned to violence in their efforts to get the political situation they want. Nationalists who believe in violence to achieve their goals are called **Republicans**. Their Unionist counterparts are called **Loyalists**.

PHOTOCALL

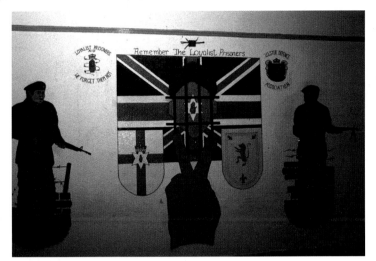

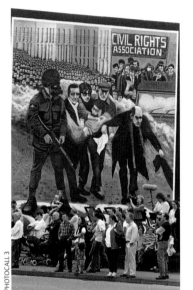

Conflict between Nationalists and Unionists has greatly influenced the way Northern Ireland is governed. When there is conflict or when political parties refuse to share power with each other, Northern Ireland is ruled directly by the British government. This is called **direct rule**. When both sides agree to share power with each other, a **power-sharing agreement** is reached between the different political parties. In this case, the British government hands back power to Northern Ireland. This power sharing government is called the **Northern Ireland Assembly** and sits in **Stormont**.

The Northern Ireland Assembly

Members of the Northern Ireland Assembly are called **Members of the Legislative Assembly (MLAs)**. Twelve ministers are chosen from the assembly. Each one is in charge of a particular department, for example education, health and agriculture. The most important ministers are the **First Minister** and the **Deputy First Minister** who are the heads of government.

FIND OUT!

Who is the current First Minister?

This assembly is responsible for areas such as health, industry and agriculture. In early 2010 an agreement was reached between parties to hand over justice and policing powers to the Northern Ireland Assembly.

The **North/South Ministerial Council** meets when there is a power sharing government. It is made up of members of the Dáil and the Northern Ireland Assembly.

The **British-Irish Council** meets when there is either divided rule or a power sharing government. Its members represent Northern Ireland, Ireland, England, Scotland, Wales, the Channel Islands and the Isle of Man.

There has been violence, conflict and bloodshed in Northern Ireland for more than four decades. Hundreds of people, many of them civilians, have lost their lives because of **'The Troubles'**. For years there have been efforts by both the British and Irish governments to bring about peace. These efforts are referred to as the **Peace Process**.

Class Discussion

1 Explain the terms Nationalist and Unionist.
2 Name the main parties in Northern Ireland.
3 Name some Northern Irish politicians you have heard of.

107

The Peace Process – The Story So Far

CAMERAPRESS

1985 **The Anglo-Irish Agreement** was signed by the leaders of both the Irish and British governments. This gave the Irish government some say in the affairs of Northern Ireland. The Unionists were unhappy with this.

1993 The Irish and British governments signed the **Downing Street Declaration**. This stated that the people of Northern Ireland should be free to decide their own future. It also invited members of the two communities to come together and find a solution to the problems in Northern Ireland.

1996 Peace talks, involving representatives from political parties, took place. These talks were chaired by the US Senator, George Mitchell. Mitchell argued that the only way forward was by non-violent means. He recommended that Loyalist and Republican groups should disarm and give up their weapons. This was called **decommissioning**. Despite this the violence continued.

1997 Talks began again between the British and Irish governments and representatives from the Nationalist and Unionist communities with a view to bringing about a lasting peace in Northern Ireland. These talks went on for a long time. During this time the IRA announcd a ceasefire.

1998 At last an agreement was reached. The British and Irish governments and representatives of the Nationalist and Unionist communities signed the **Good Friday Agreement** on 10 April. The main terms of this agreement were:
■ Northern Ireland would remain part of the United Kingdom unless a majority wished otherwise
■ Direct rule from Westminister would end. Instead a multi-party assembly would be elected to govern the state
■ A North/South Ministerial Council would be established
■ A British-Irish Council would be established.
A referendum took place to see if the people of Northern Ireland agreed with these terms. An overwhelming majority were in favour. However, a number of Loyalist and Republican groups did not decommission.

1999 After almost three decades of direct rule, power was devolved (handed over) to the new Northern Ireland Assembly. The assembly had the power to run the affairs of the health service, education and industry. Other areas, like justice and taxes, were dealt with by the British government in Westminister. The Prime Minister appointed a person to deal with Northern Ireland affairs. He or she is called the Secretary of State.

2002 After much disagreement between members of the assembly and both communities, the British government suspended the Northern Ireland Assembly and restored direct rule. Talks resumed again trying to restore the assembly.

2003 Loyalist paramilitaries announced a ceasefire.

2004 The IRA announced the end of its 'armed struggle'.

2006 The British government set the political parties in Northern Ireland a deadline to meet regarding a power-sharing agreement, otherwise direct rule would be permanent. Dialogue began between parties again.

2007 Co-operation at last. Sinn Féin agreed to recognise the **Police Service of Northern Ireland** (**PSNI**). Elections were held for the Northern Ireland Assembly and a power-sharing government ruled Northern Ireland.

2010 An agreement is reached to devolve (hand over) justice and policy powers to the Northern Ireland Assembly.

FIND OUT!

The name of the Secretary of State in Northern Ireland. The leaders of the main political parties in Northern Ireland.

ISSUE TRACKING

Events in Northern Ireland are constantly in the media. Track current events in Northern Ireland in the newspaper, radio or television.

5.3

1. A visit to:

→ The Dáil
→ The Seanad
→ Your local authority
→ A polling station
→ Áras an Uachtaráin

SKILLS YOU MIGHT USE:
→ Planning
→ Letter-writing
→ Telephone
→ Financial
→ Communication
→ Questioning
→ Reporting

2. Invite a guest speaker in to your class to find out more about the workings of democracy. The guest speaker may be:

→ A councillor
→ A government minister
→ A TD
→ The spokesperson of an interest/pressure group
→ A senior member of the civil service

SKILLS YOU MIGHT USE:
→ Letter-writing
→ Telephone
→ Hosting
→ Planning
→ Questioning
→ Listening
→ Organising

3. Organise a political awareness survey in your school to find out how aware your fellow pupils are of the political system in Ireland.

SKILLS YOU MIGHT USE:
→ Planning
→ Public relations
→ Surveying
→ Questioning
→ Organisation
→ Information gathering
→ Analysing
→ Reporting

Organise and run a mock election/referendum in your school.

SKILLS YOU MIGHT USE:
→ Planning
→ Organising
→ Communication
→ Public relations
→ Mathematical
→ Analysing
→ Reporting

CHAPTER 5.4

Democracy: International Case Studies

Case Study 1

Compulsory Voting in Australia

In Ireland, citizens do not have to vote in elections if they choose not to. However, in about twenty countries, citizens of voting age must, by law, turn up at polling stations on the day of an election. This is called **compulsory voting**. If people don't vote, they may receive a penalty, usually a fine. Even though compelled to vote, a citizen still reserves the right to spoil his or her vote. Some of the countries who operate compulsory voting at national, regional or local level include Belgium, Costa Rica, Cyprus and Switzerland.

Australia is also a country in which compulsory voting is practiced. Elections in Australia always take place on a Saturday, so that the majority of citizens are given the opportunity to vote. All citizens are required to vote unless they have a valid reason for not doing so.

If someone fails to turn up at the polling station on the day of an

election, the Australian Electoral Commission (the body in charge of elections) will write to that citizen enquiring as to why that citizen didn't vote or asking for a first

payment of $37.50, then a $75 fine. The citizen has 21 days to reply. Failure to pay the fine or supply a valid reason for not voting within 21 days means that the citizen may be brought to court and prosecuted.

Compulsory voting has proved to be a bone of contention (i.e. a topic that is passionately debated) in Australia. Those in favour of it argue that:
1. Voting is a civic duty. All citizens have a duty to vote.
2. Compulsory voting leads to high turn-out rates at election time.
3. The parliament elected truly reflects the will of the people.

Those against compulsory voting argue that:
1. It is undemocratic to force people to vote.
2. The citizen has a right not to vote.
3. Forcing a citizen to vote is an infringement of a citizen's civil liberties.

Class Discussion

1 What is compulsory voting?
2 How many countries worldwide practise compulsory voting?
3 In Australia, what happens if a citizen fails to turn up at a polling station on election day?
4 What are the arguments for and against compulsory voting?

WALKING DEBATE

Compulsory voting should be introduced in Ireland.

The following poster was produced in the run-up to the American Presidential Elections in 2004. Study the poster and answer the questions that follow.

THE POWER of **ONE VOTE** ✓

11.2.04

AMERICAN ASSOCIATION OF UNIVERSITY WOMEN

VOTER EDUCATION CAMPAIGN

800.608.5286 AAUW.ORG VOTERED@AAUW.ORG

AMERICAN ASSOCIATION OF UNIVERSITY WOMEN

QUESTIONS

1 Who produced this poster?
2 What is the key message in this poster?
3 Do you think that this poster would encourage people to vote?

GET CREATING!

Over the years many polling stations in Ireland have reported low voter turn-out during elections. Design a poster that will encourage Irish citizens to come and vote. Your poster should include a slogan and an image.

Case Study 2

Democracy in Kuwait

Kuwait is a small, oil-rich Arab state located on the Persian Gulf. Up until recently, women were not given the right to vote in elections. This is despite the fact that Kuwait was considered a democratic country. For years the Kuwaiti parliament rejected numerous bills to give women the vote. Finally, in 2005 the parliament granted equal political rights for women. These rights included the right to vote and to stand in political elections. In 2006 Dr Maasouma Al-Mubarack became the first woman cabinet minister in Kuwait.

Case Study 3

East Timor – A New Democracy

East Timor is situated in Asia, just north of Australia. For over 450 years this country has been occupied by one foreign power or another. More recently, it had been occupied by Indonesia for 25 years. During that time the East Timorese were under authoritarian rule, and therefore could not vote in elections. The people were also subjected to extreme violence and many fled their homes and became refugees in West Timor. They had no choice but to accept those in power.

However, in 1999, the Indonesian occupiers decided (under international pressure) to hold a referendum for the East Timorese people to see if the people wanted to remain under Indonesian rule or if they wanted to become an independent state. The UN supervised this referendum to ensure that the will of the people was carried out. The people voted overwhelmingly in favour of independence. East Timor became a fully independent state in May 2002. It became the 191st member of the UN in December 2002.

As a new democracy it has to face many challenges. It has to deal with extreme poverty and a large number of refugees who have returned to the state since it became a democracy. Although many challenges lie ahead for those in power, life should be better for those who live within this new democracy. They should have new opportunities in terms of education, job prospects and a safe future.

FIND OUT!

Find out more about the plight of the East Timorese people.

How is East Timor managing as one of the world's newest democracies?

Find out about the Irish bus driver, Tom Hyland, who helped bring international attention to the plight of those in East Timor.

Ideas For Taking Action

5.4

1. Conduct a survey in your school to find out if your schoolmates are in favour of compulsory voting.

SKILLS YOU MIGHT USE:
- → Organising
- → Planning
- → Communication
- → Public relations
- → Survey design
- → Analysing

2. Invite a guest speaker from a relevant organisation to find out how the lives of the East Timorese people have changed since democracy.

SKILLS YOU MIGHT USE:
- → Letter-writing
- → Communication
- → Telephone
- → Questioning
- → Hosting
- → Reporting

Democracy – Past Examination Questions

1 Complete the following sentences.
   (a) Dáil Éireann and Seanad Éireann meet in L_____ H_____.
   (b) A referendum is needed if the government wants to change the C_____.

(CSPE Paper, 2009)

2 Complete each of the following sentences.
   (a) The place where votes are cast in an election is called a p_____ s_____.
   (b) A vote to change the constitution of Ireland is called a r_____.
   (c) The Deputy Prime Minister in Ireland is known as An T_____.
   (d) The person who keeps order in Dáil Éireann during debates is called the C_____
       C_____.
   (e) Mary McAleese is the name of the P_____ of I_____.
   (f) The h_____ is the national symbol of Ireland and appears on all goverment letters
       and envelopes.

(CSPE Paper, 2008)

3 Mock General Election
   It is the year of a general election in Ireland and your class has decided to organise a mock general election.
   (a) Name and explain **TWO** activities you could undertake before carrying out a mock general election in
       order to help you understand general elections.
   (b) Design a poster that you would use to encourage students in your school to vote in the mock general
       election. As well as a drawing, your poster should include a slogan aimed at encouraging students to
       vote.
   (c) Describe **THREE** tasks that your CSPE class would have to undertake in order to organise and run a
       mock general election.

(CSPE Paper, 2007)

Website Watch
Check out the following websites for more information on the concept of democracy:

www.studentcouncil.ie
www.comhairlenanog.ie
www.president.ie
www.oireachtas.ie
www.gov.ie

TAKING ACTION

A Mock Election

Worked Example

Organising a mock election in your school is an ideal way of finding out how elections are run. It will also give you a greater understanding of the mechanics of voting. The candidates in your election do not have to be politicians. To make it more fun, your election can be for:

- The best football/GAA player
- The best film/TV star
- The best singer or band.

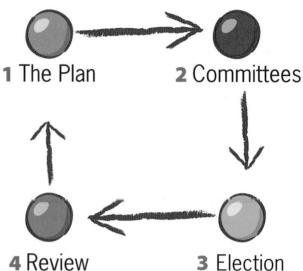

1 The Plan   2 Committees

4 Review   3 Election

Step 1: Planning
1. Who are the candidates?
2. Who will be voting?
3. Where will we hold the election?
4. What is the best time to hold the election?
5. Who do we need to help us?
6. What do we need to hold the election?

Step 2: Organising Committees
1. How many committees will we need?
2. How do we assign students to each committee?
3. What are the responsibilities of each committee?

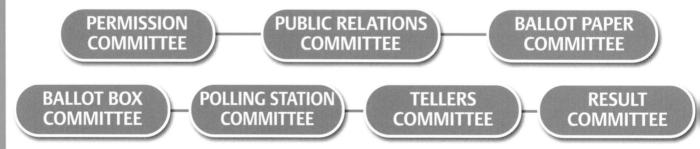

PERMISSION COMMITTEE   PUBLIC RELATIONS COMMITTEE   BALLOT PAPER COMMITTEE

BALLOT BOX COMMITTEE   POLLING STATION COMMITTEE   TELLERS COMMITTEE   RESULT COMMITTEE

The above is a list of committees that may be needed – can you think of any others?

Step 3: The Election

Step 4: The review
1. What did you learn about elections?
2. What was the voter turnout? Where you happy/disappointed with it?
3. Where you surprised about the result? What does the result tell you about the students who voted?
4. Would you do anything differently? If so, what?

Law

Laws and rules are important in any community or society. They help bring about order and lay down the ways in which individuals and groups should conduct themselves. Laws ensure that people's rights are protected and promoted. Laws also inform citizens of their responsibilities. As our communities and society change, laws also need to change from time to time.

CHAPTER 6.1

Citizenship and the Law

From the moment you woke up this morning, your actions have in some way been influenced by the law. For example, when you had your breakfast you possibly ate breakfast cereal from a package that displayed the ingredients and nutritional contents of the cereal. This information is there because a law states that it must be.

If you came to school on a bus, the law will have ensured that the bus driver had a valid licence to drive, drove on the correct side of the road and did not exceed certain speed limits. Again these are ways in which the law influences the everyday life of you, the citizen.

SHUTTERSTOCK 1, PHOTOCALL 1

The law can be described as:
'A set of rules that protects all the citizens of a country equally, giving them rights and responsibilities that everyone must respect.'

A Brief History of Irish Law

Brehon law was the original legal system in Ireland and evidence of it can be traced back to the 7th century. With the Norman invasions of the 12th century, a new form of law emerged which was based on the **feudal system**. It is these early laws that have led to many of the laws in force in Ireland today, collectively known as **common law**. Many of Ireland's laws were passed by the British Parliament while the country was under British rule.

Some of these laws have been changed, repealed or abolished since 1921 by Oireachtas Éireann. The year 1937 was a significant one for law in Ireland, as it was the year in which Bunreacht na hÉireann (the Irish Constitution) was published. As you saw previously, the Constitution sets out the fundamental law of the land and has formed the basis for the development of law in this country. It lays down the guidelines for the workings of the legal system and has had an impact on all citizens of Ireland.

The song here is often sung at sports occasions involving Irish teams. Sing it and pay careful attention to the words. It tells a story of a man breaking the law in the west of Ireland during famine times and how he was dealt with.

In 1973, Ireland joined the European Community, an event that has had an impact on some aspects of the law here. In certain cases, EU law can be more influential than Irish law. It gives certain rights to all citizens of the EU, and indeed provides a court – the European Court of Justice – to ensure citizens have access to these rights.

Laws need to be enforced and penalties need to be applied if they are to be effective. In Ireland the responsibility for enforcing the law generally lies with An Garda Síochána. The courts have the powers to implement penalties.

PHOTOCALL

The Fields of Athenry

An Irish folk song of oppression and cruelty

By Pete St. John

By a lonely prison wall
I heard a young girl calling:
'Michael they have taken you away
For you stole Trevallyn's corn
So the young might see the morn
Now the prison ship lies waiting in the bay.'

Refrain:
Low lie the Fields of Athenry
Where once we watched the small free birds fly
Our love was on the wing
We had dreams and songs to sing
It's so lonely round the Fields of Athenry.

By a lonely prison wall
I heard a young man calling:
'Nothing matters Mary when you're free
Against the famine and the crown
I rebelled - they ran me down
Now you must raise our child with dignity.'

Refrain:
By a lonely harbour wall
She watched the last star falling
As that prison ship sailed out against the sky.
Sure she'll wait and hope and pray
For her love in Botany Bay.
It's lonely round the Fields of Athenry.

Talking Point

1. In 'The Fields of Athenry' a father is deported to far-off Australia for stealing corn from a rich landowner to feed his starving family. Do you think that this would happen in Ireland today? Why or why not?
2. Are today's laws fair? Give reasons for your answer.
3. Name one law that you would change and say why.
4. Name one law that you think is fair and should not be changed. Say why.

How Does The Law Affect Citizens?

Group Discussion

Divide the class into small groups to discuss the following before reporting back to the class as a whole:
How does the law affect the following people?

 A farmer   **A publican**   **A teacher**   **A bank official**   **A politician**   **A pensioner**

Clearly, therefore, laws affect all types of citizens in both similar and different ways. As a Junior Certificate student, your life is affected by various laws and rules, all of which have been passed by adults! Do you think this is fair? Should younger people have a say in making laws? List some ways in which they could do so.

Here are some examples of laws that affect you:

- You must attend school until you are 16 years of age
- You may not buy cigarettes until you are 16
- You may not buy/consume alcohol until you are 18
- You may not drive a car until you are 17
- You may not be in a public house after 9pm until you are 18
- You may not stand for election to the Dáil until you are 18
- You may not vote in local, national or European elections.

Can you think of other laws or rules that have an impact on your life? Which ones would you change and why?

Talking Point

1 Do you think that the legal voting age should be changed from 18 years to 16 years? Why or why not? Suggest how you would go about getting the voting age law changed. What process would you go through?
2 Looking at the school community, you will probably conclude that the laws that govern the school community are not always fair. Many people might well agree with you, but how would you change them and still keep order in the school environment?

Times change and laws change with them. The following is a list of laws that have changed in the recent past:

- Smoking in the workplace banned
- Seat belts compulsory for every passenger in all cars
- Being born in Ireland no longer entitles one to automatic citizenship
- Under 18s are not permitted in pubs after 9pm.

When Law Breaks Down
Magician Barry's grandfather dies after Waterford attack

The grandfather of magician Keith Barry has died in hospital from injuries he sustained during a burglary at his home in Waterford last week. Eighty-four-year-old Paddy Barry suffered serious head and facial injuries, as well as a broken arm, when he was attacked by three men who called to his home on Mount Sion Avenue last Wednesday evening.

He had been unresponsive since the attack and died in hospital at 5.30am today. A post-mortem will be carried out to determine whether he died as a direct result of his injuries.

A man who was arrested by gardaí in relation to the incident was released. A garda spokesman said a file has been prepared for the Director of Public Prosecutions.

Mr Barry had lived in the Mount Sion Avenue area of Waterford for 60 years.

PHOTOCALL

At the time, his devastated grandson Keith, who has staged sell-out shows in Las Vegas, hit out at the justice system and said other pensioners living in the quiet part of the city were petrified. He called for mandatory three-year prison sentences for criminals who break into pensioners' homes.

'I think anybody who enters a pensioner's home uninvited — that's anybody over 65 — it should be a mandatory sentence, without bail, without excuses,' said the entertainer last week. 'These thugs have no fear. They have no fear for the law, they have no fear for the justice system and they have no fear of us in our homes.'

Gardaí have appealed for anyone with information to come forward.

(Source: www.breakingnews.ie 22/09/2009)

WALKING DEBATE

This attack on an elderly member of society was shocking. In the passage, Keith Barry says the law is too soft and people who commit such awful crimes do so because they have no fear of the law.

Organise a walking debate based on the motion:
The justice system is too soft on people who break into pensioners' homes.

ISSUE TRACKING

As a homework exercise, track any issues relating to lawlessness from a local or a national newspaper. Cut out the article and bring it to your next CSPE class for discussion.

IMAGINE!

Imagine that you have been stranded on a desert island with ten other people. You have radio contact, but because of storms and high seas a ship cannot reach you for a week. There are limited supplies of food, water and firewood. You have been elected leader of the group and have been given the responsibility of laying down rules for the group.

What five rules or laws would you make to ensure the health and safety of the group?

Wordsearch on Citizenship and the Law

Complete the word search below

H	C	A	X	T	L	N	J	V	S	S	N	P	S	V
L	I	R	B	A	N	U	W	Y	H	O	F	R	E	V
J	I	U	G	O	S	O	O	C	I	M	H	O	L	K
Y	D	E	Y	T	L	P	H	T	X	V	O	T	U	Y
C	L	N	I	K	V	I	U	E	M	K	P	E	R	X
R	Q	C	A	Q	K	T	S	P	R	R	E	C	P	X
I	E	S	Q	O	I	B	F	H	O	B	C	T	X	M
M	G	K	V	T	L	X	K	E	E	C	O	U	R	T
E	L	Q	S	Z	K	G	B	R	X	D	K	W	O	K
N	G	N	C	I	T	I	Z	E	N	S	H	I	P	Y
M	O	A	P	J	J	H	W	O	D	Q	N	B	N	R
C	W	P	R	I	L	E	L	A	A	A	I	Z	H	V
B	M	X	X	D	M	N	F	D	V	Y	U	S	D	C
E	I	F	I	N	A	M	K	B	X	A	Z	X	R	Y
E	C	R	O	F	N	E	T	G	C	P	O	W	E	U

- ABOLISHED
- BREHON
- CITIZENSHIP
- CONSTITUTION
- COURT
- CRIME
- ENFORCE
- GARDA
- JUSTICE
- LEGAL
- PROTECT
- RULES

Ideas For Taking Action

6.1

→ Carry out a survey on whether or not pupils agree with certain rules in your school.

→ Draw up a charter of rules for your class. You might decide to do this with some help from your teacher and the student council. Try and keep the list to a maximum of ten rules which should be easily understood. It might also be a good idea to have rewards available if the class follows the rules. Unfortunately you may also have to think of some punishments for those not following the rules!

SKILLS YOU MIGHT USE:
→ Questioning
→ Designing a questionnaire
→ Negotiating
→ Presentation
→ Listening
→ ICT

Can you think of other skills that you may need to undertake this action?

Law at the Local Level

FIND OUT!

Are you familiar with any of the bye-laws in your community? Name some of these bye-laws and state what you think of them.

As members of our local community, we are bound by European, national and local laws. We will look at national and European law in more detail in chapters 6.3 and 6.4, so now we'll concentrate on aspects of **local law**.

As we saw in Section 5, each local authority has specific duties and responsibilities. Among these are making sure that people obey laws that have been passed at national level. Local authorities may also enforce **bye-laws**. Bye-laws are laws which are put in place to look after the needs of a specific area. They may not be law in other areas. For example, some local authorities introduce laws banning pets in local public parks, while other local authorities do not. In most cases these laws are implemented by employees of the local community – community wardens and members of An Garda Síochána.

In general bye-laws will vary from community to community. However, many will have bye-laws based on some or all of the following:

→ Planning

→ Parking

→ Traffic

→ Litter

→ Control of animals

PHOTOCALL 4, SHUTTERSTOCK 1

Case Study

National Law at the Local Level

Your local authority has a responsibility to enforce laws that have been passed in various acts by the Oireachtas. We will now look at one particular example of this – the Litter Pollution Act.

The Litter Pollution Act 1997 [as amended by the Waste Management Act 2001 and the Protection of The Environment Act 2003] brought in heavy penalties to tackle the litter pollution problem in Ireland. Your local authority is responsible for the litter laws in your community. The local authority has to bring in measures to prevent litter and also has the power to take action against citizens who break or ignore these laws.

Under current legislation, leaving or throwing litter in a public place is an offence that can be subject to an on-the-spot fine of €125 or a maximum fine of €3,000 if a person is convicted of a litter offence in the District Court (your local court). Heavier fines may be applied to persistent offenders.

The local authority appoints Litter Wardens to monitor and implement this law, but members of An Garda Síochána may also apply on-the-spot fines. If a person is convicted of an offence, then he or she may also have to pay the local authority's costs and expenses in investigating the offence and the costs of going to court.

Private homes, businesses and areas of public access are also monitored by the local authority under this act. It also applies to dog owners. They must remove their pet's waste from public places and dispose of it in a proper manner.

PHOTOCALL, SHUTTERSTOCK

When Law Breaks Down in the Community

Sometimes people in communities feel that they need to stand up to those who break the law. In communities where inhabitants feel intimidated and afraid, they take matters into their own hands and organise themselves to fight back against criminals.

WALKING DEBATE

Meetings like the one advertised in this poster are a good idea.

Anti-Social Behaviour

Intimidation
Wilful destruction
of people's property
voice your views

Community Centre
Tues 8 O'clock Aug 29th

Not my problem

Then wait until you and yours are

Attacked

Death and Destruction in Northern Ireland

For many years during 'The Troubles', the people in Northern Ireland suffered from a breakdown in law. One of the worst atrocities to happen in Northern Ireland was the Omagh bombing.

On 15 August 1998 at 3.10 pm, a car bomb exploded in the busy town of Omagh, Co. Tyrone. It killed 29 people and seriously injured many more. A group known as the 'Real' IRA carried out this atrocity. They claimed it was a part of the ongoing war against the British in Northern Ireland. However, the view of most people was that it was a pathetic excuse for mass murder.

FIND OUT!

Check out your local library or internet sources for more information about the breakdown of law during 'The Troubles' in Northern Ireland.

Could It Happen Again?

The Omagh bombing did help to speed up the Peace Process in Northern Ireland. Today, Northern Ireland is a more peaceful society, but we must always be aware that certain individuals in society will disregard the law. The Police Service of Northern Ireland (PSNI) and An Garda Síochana in the Republic of Ireland work very hard to enforce the law on our island to make sure we do not have another bombing like that in Omagh.

Knife Crime in Ireland – a Growing Problem

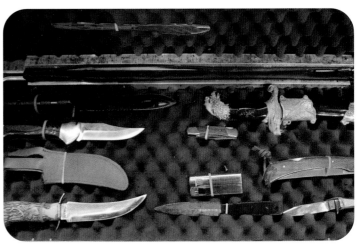

Knife crime has become a horrific problem in our society in recent years. Stabbings in the country now are responsible for dozens of deaths every year. Many people have blamed this rise in knife crime on a reduction in the sentences handed out to the perpetrators. Is the law not working?

In June 2008 one of Ireland's most experienced judges – Mr Justice Paul Carney – spoke of his annoyance at the Court of Criminal Appeal reducing sentences for knife crime. In one case, he said, a twenty-year sentence was cut to just eight years, while in another, a fourteen-year sentence was also reduced to eight years. He stated that in any crime where a knife is used and a life is taken, the minimum sentence should be twenty years and should not be reduced.

It would appear that more and more stabbings are happening as a result of young people being under the influence of alcohol and drugs. The problem also has increased due to the attitude of some young people who think that it is either cool to carry a knife or that it is needed as a form of defence.

Class Discussion

1 Is the law working in the case of knife crime?
2 Why was the judge annoyed with the Court of Criminal Appeal?
3 How could the law help to reduce knife crime?
4 Why do some young people carry knives?
5 Do you think that the problem can be reduced? How?

The Role of the Community Garda

The Community Garda plays a special role in your community. The Community Garda carries out many of the same tasks that other Gardaí do, but also has extra responsibilities. One of the main functions of a Community Garda is to get to know the different groups working in the community. Developing links with local businesses, youth workers, sports clubs and other voluntary organisations is an important aspect of the job.

Young people and the elderly are often the most vulnerable groups in society and the Community Garda spends a lot of time meeting these people. For example, the Garda Schools Programme was set up to create a link between the Community Garda and schools and pupils. It covers many things, including road safety, personal safety and the role of the Gardaí. Community Gardaí have visited CSPE classes throughout the country in the course of their work.

PHOTOCALL

Ideas For Taking Action

6.2

→ If you are unfamiliar with local law, why not organise a visit to your local authority to investigate aspects of local law?

→ Your class could arrange for a Community Garda to visit your class and discuss issues of law and lawlessness in your community.

SKILLS YOU MIGHT USE:
→ Letter-writing
→ Information gathering
→ Questioning
→ Hosting
→ Communication
→ Listening

Can you think of other skills that you may need to undertake this action?

Irish Law – Some Key Aspects

As members of a school community, you are expected to observe certain rules and regulations. In addition, you have a responsibility towards the other members of the school community and to the school environment itself. For example, you must begin class at a particular time and you must have respect for school property.

As Irish citizens there are also certain rules and laws we must observe and obey. As we have seen, the basic laws of Ireland are laid down in Ireland's constitution, Bunreacht na hÉireann. These laws are enforced with the help of the Garda Síochána, the defence forces and the courts.

Who Makes the Law?

Laws are made by governments, but before they can be introduced, they have to go through a number of steps or stages.

Step 1: A new law is proposed. It is known as a **Bill**. A Bill can stem from either Dáil Éireann or the Seanad, but in most cases they are introduced in the Dáil. A copy of the Bill is circulated to TDs for analysis and discussion.

Step 2: After discussion and debate, TDs suggest **amendments** (changes) to the Bill.

Step 3: The Bill is presented to a **Special Committee** that examines the Bill very closely and discusses it further.

Step 4: The Bill is amended and rewritten. This is called the **report stage**. This is the final draft of the Bill. No more changes can take place.

Step 5: The amended Bill goes back to the Dáil and is discussed further. If the Bill is passed, it is sent to the Seanad for further debate. To become law, the Bill must be passed by both the Dáil and the Seanad.

Step 6: The Bill must be signed by the President. Only then can it become law.

Step 7: Upon the President's signature, the Bill becomes an **Act**.

Class Discussion

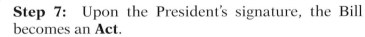

1 What is a proposed law called?
2 Describe the stages a Bill must go through before it becomes an Act.
3 Why, do you think, does a Bill have to be passed by both the Dáil and the Seanad?
4 Find out how rules are made in your school.

Enforcing the Law

Failure to obey laws means that you are breaking them. If you **break the law** you may be penalised or punished in some way.

Three institutions have been put in place to protect Irish citizens and discourage them from breaking the law. These are
- An Garda Síochána
- The Defence Forces
- The Courts.

Together, these institutions collectively enforce the law.

An Garda Síochána

An Garda Síochána or 'Guardians of the Peace' are the country's national police service. They are responsible for maintening law and order. Their mission is to provide the highest possible standards of:

- Community commitment
- Personal protection
- State security.

There are over 14,000 Gardaí stationed in approximately 700 stations all over Ireland. The management and control of the Gardaí is the responsibility of the **Garda Commissioner**. He or she is appointed by the government and is answerable to the **Department of Justice, Equality and Law Reform**.

The Gardaí are one of the few police forces in the world who carry out their day-to-day duties unarmed. These duties include:

- Enforcement of road traffic laws

- Responding to calls for assistance in road accidents, burglaries, incidences of crime and vandalism, and domestic violence

- Prevention and investigation of drug-related offences

- The maintenance of state security.

In recent years the Gardaí have forged closer links with communities. These links have been strengthened with the introduction of crime prevention schemes such as **Neighbourhood Watch** and **Community Alert**. In addition, most stations have a **Community Garda** who liaises with community representatives to discuss issues of mutual interest. These schemes enable citizens to become actively involved in the maintenance of law and order within their communities.

Student Task

1 How many Gardaí are there in Ireland?
2 Who is responsible for the management of the Gardaí? To whom are they answerable?
3 What are the main responsibilities of a Garda?
4 In what ways have the Gardaí tried to forge links with their communities?

PHOTOCALL. POSED BY MODEL.

Questions

1 Do you think that a law might have been broken in this photograph? What law?
2 Why are such laws important?
3 Suggest some ways in which laws could be changed to improve road safety.
4 How could CSPE students learn more about laws concerning road safety?
5 Imagine that you are the Minister for Justice, Equality and Law Reform. Describe what you would do to ensure that the law is enforced properly on Irish roads.

FIND OUT!

1. What is the name of the Garda Commissioner?
2. Who is the current Minister of Justice, Equality and Law Reform?
3. Gather information about a Neighbourhood Watch or Community Alert Scheme in your area.

The Defence Forces

The Irish Defence Forces consist of the Permanent Defence Forces and the Reserve Defence Forces (FCA). There are over 10,000 men and women employed in the Defence Forces today. Their roles are:

- To defend the state against armed aggression
- To assist the Garda Síochána when requested
- To participate in multinational peace support and humanitarian relief operations in conjunction with the United Nations
- To provide a fishery protection service
- To carry out other duties such as search and rescue, air ambulance service, assistance on the occasion of natural or other disasters.

The Permanent Defence Forces consist of:

1 The Army
2 The Naval Service
3 The Air Corps.

PHOTOCALL 2

The Law in Ireland

Irish law can be broadly divided into two types: – civil law and criminal law.

Civil Law

Civil law is concerned with disputes between **private individuals**. It may involve a case being taken against an individual, a business or an organisation. These cases are called **civil actions**. Civil law also deals with certain personal issues such as divorce, adoption or making a will.

A common type of civil action involves personal injury claims. If, for example, someone is knocked down by a car and injured, that individual, by law, is entitled to seek compensation from the car driver. The judge, presiding over the case, must decide if the victim is entitled to compensation and if so, how much. Civil actions can also arise from disputes over planning permission, rights of way and breach of contract. There is usually no jury in civil cases. The outcome of these cases is decided solely by a judge.

Criminal Law

Criminal law deals with serious offences such as assault, armed robbery, theft, rape and murder. Unlike civil law, the state brings the case against individuals suspected of serious crimes. The person responsible for all criminal law cases in Ireland is the **Director of Public Prosecutions**. If the accused is found guilty of a serious crime, he or she might be fined or given a jail sentence. It is the responsibility of a jury, under the direction of a judge, to decide the facts of a case and return its verdict on whether an individual is guilty or not guilty.

FIND OUT

The name of the current Director of Public Prosecutions in Ireland.

Student Task

Study the list below and state whether each is a civil law or criminal law matter.

- Drug pushing
- Stealing
- Seeking a divorce
- Adoption
- Injury from a car crash
- Murder
- Breach of contract
- Drink-driving
- Land dispute

The Courts

There are several different types of courts. Look at the diagram below to see how they are organised.

PHOTOCALL

CRIMINAL LAW	CIVIL LAW
THE COURTS	THE COURTS
Supreme Court	Supreme Court
Court of Criminal Appeal	
Central Criminal Court	High Court
Special Criminal Court	
Circuit Court	Circuit Court
District Court	District Court

The District Court

The District Court hears civil cases, covering such things as family law cases (barring orders and custody of children), liquor licensing laws and civil actions where the compensation awarded does not exceed €6,350. It also deals with criminal cases such as driving offences, theft and assault. There are twenty-three such courts throughout Ireland. There is only one judge presiding over these cases and there is no jury. If an individual is unhappy with the outcome of a case, he or she can make an appeal to its higher court – the Circuit Court.

The Circuit Court

The Circuit Court also deals with civil and criminal cases. There are eight circuit courts in Ireland. This court also deals with matters relating to family law, and deals with civil actions in which compensation does not exceed €38,000. The circuit court is also responsible for dealing with more serious criminal matters such as armed robbery. If individuals are unhappy with the outcome of a case, they can appeal to the High Court.

The High Court

The High Court is situated in the Four Courts in Dublin. It deals with civil actions where the compensation is greater than €38,000. It also deals with the most serious criminal cases such as rape and murder and is known as the Central Criminal Court. Because of the seriousness of these offences, a judge and jury must decide the outcome of a case. This court also hears appeals from the lower courts.

The Four Courts

The Special Criminal Court

This court tries individuals who have breached the **Offences Against The State Act**. An example of an offence under this law includes membership of an unlawful organisation, for example the IRA. In recent years this court has also dealt with cases concerned with drugs. Three judges preside over these cases and there is no jury.

Can you suggest a reason why there is no jury?

The Court of Criminal Appeal

If an individual is convicted of a criminal offence in the Circuit Court, Central Criminal Court or the Special Criminal Court, they have a right to appeal. These appeals are heard in this court.

The Supreme Court

This is the highest and most important court in Ireland. This court hears appeals from the High Court. The President may refer a Bill to this court to determine if it is unconstitutional. Usually, in this situation, there are five judges and no jury. In most cases, an individual is unable to appeal the decision of the Supreme Court. Appeals can only be made when a decision is deemed to be in breach of European law.

All of the above courts deal with citizens over 16 years of age. Offenders below that age are tried in the **Children's Court**. There is no jury in this court and cases are heard in-camera, which means they are held in private. This is to protect the identity of the child.

Group Activity

Divide the class into five groups. Each group will make a report on a 'case' they have been following in any one of the following courts:

1. District Court
2. Circuit Court
3. High Court
4. Special Criminal Court
5. Supreme Court.

Inside a Courtroom: Cast of Characters

Judge

Jury

Solicitor

Barrister

Stenographer

Witness

1 **Judge:** The judge is in charge during a court case. He or she instructs a jury on legal issues and decides if the accused is guilty or innocent. When a citizen is found to have broken the law, the judge decides the punishment.

2 **Jury:** A jury is a panel of twelve men and women who are selected at random from the electoral register. All jury members must be over 18. On hearing the evidence presented in the case, the jury must decide the outcome.

3 **Solicitor:** Most citizens, when brought to court, hire the services of a solicitor. He or she prepares the case for trial and chooses a barrister to present the case in court.

4 **Barrister:** The barrister presents the case in court. Barristers are easy to recognise because they wear a gown and wig. They can either prosecute or defend an individual in court.

5 **Stenographer:** The stenographer must take a note of all that is said in court.

6 **Witness:** Witnesses are brought to court to give their side of the story. They may be cross-examined by the opposing party.

Crime and Punishment

Citizens found guilty of breaking the law must be punished or penalised in some way. The punishment will depend on the seriousness of the crime. For less serious crimes, an individual may receive:

- A caution
- Penalty points on his or her driving licence, or an endorsement
- A fine
- Community service.

However, more serious crimes, such as armed robbery and murder, will receive more severe punishments. An individual guilty of these crimes will receive a jail sentence and be sent to prison.

Inside a Prison – a Student's Perspective

This is a description, written by a 3rd year CSPE student, of his visit to Mountjoy prison, Dublin

As part of our action project my class decided to visit Mountjoy Jail. We had all heard stories about the easy life prisoners have so we decided to visit the jail to see first-hand how prisoners live. As a class we divided into a number of committees in order to prepare for the visit. **The contact committee** rang the governor's office in Mountjoy to arrange a date for the visit. The **permission committee** drafted a letter to the principal to seek his permission for the visit. When we got the go-ahead we had to arrange transport to and from the prison. This was the responsibility of the **transport committee**. There were many questions we wanted to ask about prison life, so a **questions committee** drew up a list of questions to put to the prison officers who showed us around.

On the day of the visit, we were met at the gate of the men's prison by two prison officers. They lay down the ground rules and got each of us to sign in. Security was very tight. We were first brought into a visiting room where prisoners can meet their friends and family. The visiting room was very basic. It consisted of two long benches divided by a long sheet of perspex glass. Video cameras were in operation. The prison officer explained that drugs are often smuggled into prisons in this room, even though a number of prison guards are present. The prison officers explained that

each prisoner is allowed one 30-minute visit a week. The prisoner can only nominate six people he wants to visit him. However, there is no limit on the number of children that can visit the prisoner. We found out that Mountjoy is a medium-security closed prison with a bed capacity of over 450.

We then entered the main prison. The first thing that hit us was how old the prison looks. We learned that the first prisoners were admitted here around 1850 and the prison certainly hasn't changed much since then. We were then brought into a wing in the prison. The prison has different wings for different categories of prisoners. We were shown the inside of a cell. It was very small with just a bed and a shelf in it. We learned that most prisoners are locked in their cells for sleeping, eating and drinking. They are only allowed out to 'slop out' or get their meals. Meals must be eaten in the cell. Some prisoners are involved in educational programmes, studying for their Junior Cert and Leaving Cert. Some are even studying for their degrees!

We were then taken to the exercise yard which is very basic by all accounts. The yard was quite small with 'goalposts' painted on the walls. We soon realised that the stories about a life of luxury behind prison walls are untrue. Our final port of call on our visit was the execution room, where in the past

prisoners were executed by hanging. A famous Irishman, Kevin Barry, was executed in this room. As the death penalty has been abolished in Ireland, the room is not used anymore.

When we left the prison that day, many in the class were in shock at what they saw and we all agreed that we would not like to set foot in there again. When we returned to school the **report committee** made out a report outlining what we had learned from our visit. The poster committee made posters highlighting some of the sights we had seen in the prison. We hung them on the classroom wall. All in the class agreed that our visit to Mountjoy Jail proved a valuable experience.

WALKING DEBATE

Prisons are not the answer to dealing with criminals.

Consumer Law

On your way to school this morning, the chances are that you went into a shop to buy your lunch or something you needed for school. When you buy goods or a service (a haircut, for example), you are considered to be a **consumer**. As a consumer you are entitled to certain rights and these rights are protected by law. There are more than sixty pieces of consumer legislation in Ireland, but perhaps the main law that affects you as a consumer is the **Sale of Goods and Services Act, 1980**. Under this Act goods purchased by a consumer must:

- Be of a reasonable quality
- Fit for the purpose for which they are intended
- Be as described in advertising or labelling.

If the goods purchased do not live up to these standards, by law the goods must be either repaired or replaced by the retailer. The consumer may also be entitled to a refund.

If the consumer avails of a service the following applies:

- The service provider must have the skill to provide the service
- The service is provided with care and diligence
- The service is of a high standard and quality.

If a consumer is unhappy with a service, he or she may be entitled to some form of compensation.

Consumers can contact the **Office of the Director of Consumer Affairs** for advice on consumer matters. If a consumer feels that his or her rights are not being met they can bring a retailer or a service provider to the **Small Claims Court**. This service is provided by the Disctrict Court. Its aim is to provide an inexpensive, fast and easy way for consumers to resolve disputes without the need to employ a solicitor.

Case Study

Read the extract below and answer the questions that follow.

Mary McCarthy's Holiday Hell

Mary McCarthy browsed through the pages of the holiday brochure. One particular hotel in Lanzarote caught her eye. The advert read: 'Four Star Luxury Hotel. All rooms with stunning sea views. Self Catering €499, Half Board €599 for one week.' This sounded great! Mary went to her travel agent, Happy Holidays, and booked a one-week holiday on a half-board basis. The day before the holiday, she bought a long-life suitcase which cost her €99 in Murphy's Store. She was all set for her holiday.

After a four-hour flight, Mary arrived in Lanzarote airport and went to the baggage carousel to collect her suitcase. At last she

spotted it – without a handle. 'Long-life indeed!' Mary thought. After lugging her suitcase to the transfer bus, and a short journey, Mary arrived at her hotel. To her amazement she saw only three stars above the hotel name. She told the holiday rep that she had paid for a four-star, luxury hotel,

but the rep said there was nothing he could do.

Feeling angry, Mary trawled her suitcase to her room and opened the curtains. There in front of her stood a large grey concrete wall. '"Sea view" my eye!' she yelled, the veins standing out in her forehead. Feeling angry and tired, she went down to the restaurant for a well-needed meal. When she ordered her food, she was informed by the waiter that she was only booked in on a bed-and-breakfast basis so he couldn't serve her. Despite her pleas, Mary had to leave the restaurant. She was tired, hungry and extremely angry! This was certainly the holiday from hell!

Questions

1 What standards did the suitcase not live up to? Is Mary entitled to any redress for this? If so, what?
2 Did the holiday live up to its description? In what ways did it, and in what ways did it not?
3 Do you think that Mary is entitled to any compensation for her holiday from hell?
4 If Mary doesn't receive compensation from the travel agency, what are her options?
5 Pretend that you are Mary McCarthy. Compose a letter of complaint to the travel agency.

The Office of the Ombudsman

Set up in 1984, the role of the **Office of the Ombudsman** is to deal with complaints made by members of the public about how they have been treated by public bodies such as hospitals, government departments, local authorities or An Post. The ombudsman will fully investigate the complaint and make a decision on it as well as enforcing consumer law.

Office of the Ombudsman
Oifig an Ombudsman

Emily O'Reilly, the current Ombudsman

The National Consumer Agency

Established by the Irish government in 2007, this agency defends the interests of consumers. It represents the voice of the consumer, offers education and information services for consumers, and is responsible for enforcing consumer law. Some key consumer tips:

1 Always ask for a receipt.
2 If you have a complaint, act quickly.
3 You are not entitled to a refund if you simply change your mind.

national **consumer** agency
gníomhaireacht náisiúnta **tomhaltóirí**

putting **consumers** first

*Ann Fitzgerald,
CEO of The National Consumer Agency*

This agency also has its own website at **www.consumerconnect.ie** where consumers can access a wide variety of tips and information concerning consumer law.

Class Discussion

1 What is the role of the Office of the Ombudsman?
2 Is there a need for the National Consumer Agency? Why?
3 What are the main pieces of advice the National Consumer Agency gives to consumers? Is it good advice?

ROLE PLAY

You have just purchased a top-of-the-range DVD player. When you get it home, you discover that it is not working. Compose a dialogue of what happens when you return to the shop with the damaged goods. The cast of characters might include you - the consumer, a shop assistant and a manager. Choose two classmates to act out the roles with you.

6.3

1. Visits

Organise a visit to a prison or the local court.

SKILLS YOU MIGHT USE:

→ Letter-writing
→ Telephone
→ Planning
→ Financing
→ Organising
→ Questioning
→ Reporting

2. Guest Speakers

Invite someone employed in the legal profession to come and address your class about their work.

SKILLS YOU MIGHT USE:

→ Letter-writing
→ Telephone
→ Planning
→ Communication
→ Hosting
→ Questioning
→ Listening
→ Reporting

3. Crime Survey

Get together in groups and brainstorm how you could perform a crime survey among the pupils at your school.

SKILLS YOU MIGHT USE:

→ Survey design
→ Computer
→ Questioning
→ Public relations
→ Information gathering
→ Analysing
→ Reporting

Can you think of other skills that you may need to undertake this action?

Law – an International Dimension

We are not only Irish citizens, but also global citizens – citizens of the world. As a result, we are subject to international laws. These laws ensure that the rights of citizens throughout the world are protected.

What is International Law?

CAMERAPRESS

International law is concerned with the relationships between states or countries. A body of law exists that countries all over the world must observe. These laws include economic laws, environmental laws, criminal laws and laws relating to human rights issues. Under international law, states are given certain rights, which, in turn, protect the citizens of those states. In addition, states also have certain responsibilities or duties towards other states or countries.

International law as we know it today can be traced back to the establishment of the United Nations at the end of the Second World War. In 1949, the United Nations drafted a **Declaration on the Rights and Duties of States**. This declaration means that every state has:

- The right to independence
- The right to choose its own government
- A responsibility not to start wars with other states
- The right to treat all persons equally regardless of religion, gender, language or race
- A responsibility to settle disputes with other states by peaceful means.

Under international law, anyone who commits a crime is liable to be punished. This means a head of state such as a president or prime minister can be punished if found guilty. The most serious crimes committed under international law include:

1 **Crimes against peace**: this crime is committed when one state starts a war of aggression on another state. It can also include the breaking of peace treaties.

2 **War crimes**: these crimes include ill-treatment of prisoners of war, hostage-taking and the plunder of both private and public property during a war.

3 **Crimes against humanity**: these involve crimes against civilians during a war between two or more states or during a period of civil strife within a state. These crimes are usually committed on racial or religious grounds and can include genocide or 'ethnic cleansing'.

Questions

1 Why do we have international law?
2 From your knowledge of history, can you think of any crimes that were punishable under international law?
3 Can you think of any crimes that are being committed currently under international law?
4 Find out about the Nuremburg Trials. Your history teacher may be able to give you information on this.

Who Makes International Laws?

Most international law is made by the United Nations. The UN has a membership of 192 countries. It has set up a special body called the **International Law Commission** to create and develop international laws. This commission has 34 members who meet every year to develop existing laws or create new ones. Every member of the UN has a right to make recommendations and have their views on new or existing laws heard.

The International Court of Justice

The International Court of Justice is the most important international court. Situated in The Hague in the Netherlands, and established by the United Nations in 1946, the role of this court is to settle disputes between states and to offer advice and opinions on legal matters. Some of the most common cases brought to this court include disputes over territory, arguments over land and maritime boundaries and violations of trade agreements. It also deals with aspects of both criminal and human rights law. Fifteen judges are elected to this court from various countries.

The International Criminal Court

This court tries individuals for the most serious crimes. It is also situated in The Hague, and deals with individuals suspected of committing war crimes or crimes against humanity. The first head of state to be brought before this court was Slobodan Milosevic, erstwhile President of former Yugoslavia, who was suspected of directing and encouraging war crimes and crimes against humanity against the ethnic Albanian civilians in Kosovo.

The Death Penalty - An International Issue

Some countries in the world punish individuals convicted of serious crimes, such as murder, by administering the death penalty. This is also called **capital punishment**. The most common methods of administering the death penalty are by way of the electric chair, lethal injection and hanging. In Saudi Arabia, a country which still retains the death penalty, beheading is the favoured form of execution. Ireland abolished the death penalty in 1990. The last person to be executed in Ireland was Michael Manning. He was convicted of murder and hanged in Mountjoy Prison in 1924.

Although the death penalty has been abolished in Ireland, almost half the countries in the world still retain it. The majority of executions in recent times have taken place in the US, China and Saudi Arabia. In the US alone there are almost 3,000 prisoners awaiting execution on the infamous Death Row.

The death penalty has always been a contentious issue. Those in favour feel it acts as a deterrent for serious crimes, such as murder. They believe in the saying: 'an eye for an eye, a tooth for a tooth'. Others, however, believe that the death penalty is a barbaric method of punishment that strips an individual of his or her human dignity. People who feel that the death penalty should be abolished are known as **abolitionists**. Organisations such as Amnesty International have worked tirelessly for the abolition of the death penalty.

CAMERAPRESS 2, CORBIS 1, ALAMY 1, TOPFOTO 1

WALKING DEBATE

The death penalty should be reinstated in Ireland.

YOUR CALL!

Do you think that the death penalty should be abolished worldwide? Write a speech outlining your views.

6.4

1 Invite a guest speaker into your class to discuss various aspects of the law. Possible speakers might include:

→ a solicitor
→ a local TD
→ a barrister
→ a county councillor
→ a judge
→ a representative from Amnesty International
→ a human rights worker
→ a Community Garda
→ a member of the defence forces

SKILLS YOU MIGHT USE:

→ Letter-writing
→ Questioning
→ Communications
→ Information gathering
→ Hosting
→ Listening

2 Visit a local courthouse to explore how courts operate. You might even like to visit a prison to see what life is like behind bars.

3 Carry out a survey in your school to find out the number of students in your school who have been affected by crime.

4 Organise a petition calling for the abolition of the death penalty. When you have a large number of signatures, send it to an embassy of a country that still retains capital punishment.

SKILLS YOU MIGHT USE:

→ Organising
→ Surveying
→ Analysing
→ Listening
→ Negotiating
→ Letter-writing

Can you think of other skills that you may need to undertake this action?

Law - Sample Examination Questions

1 Complete each of the following sentences:

(i) B_____ na h_____ is the basis for the development of law in Ireland.

(ii) _____ laws are laws which are put in place to look after the needs of a specific area.

(iii) A new law which is proposed is called a _____.

(iv) The management and control of the Garda Siochana is the responsibility of the G_____ C_____.

(v) The highest court in Ireland is called the _____ court.

(vi) The person responsible for all criminal law cases in Ireland is the D_____ of P_____ P_____ .

(vii) The person who presents a case in court is called a b_____ .

(viii) A consumer who needs advice can get it from the office of the D _____ of C_____ A_____ .

2 As part of your learning about law, your class has decided to organise a visit to a court house or a prison to see the Irish justice system in action.

(i) Name **three** committees and describe the work each of these would do to plan and organise the visit.

(ii) In order to help your understanding of the concept of law, write down **three** questions you would ask your guide.

(iii) Name and describe **two** follow-up activities that your class could undertake as result of the visit.

Website Watch

Check out the following websites that can give you more information on the concept of law:

www.military.ie	www.irishprisons.ie
www.rdf.ie	www.crimecouncil.gov.ie
www.courts.ie	www.consumerassociation.ie
www.justice.ie	www.ombudsman.gov.ie
www.garda.ie	

TAKING ACTION

A Community Garda addresses our class

Inviting a guest speaker to your class is often a great way to develop your understanding of an issue. Many communities have a designated Community Garda who would be willing to speak to your class on legal issues and on the role of the Gardaí.

It is very important that the class plans the visit carefully and that all students are involved in some way. The best way to do this is to agree on a plan of action and divide the class into various committees.

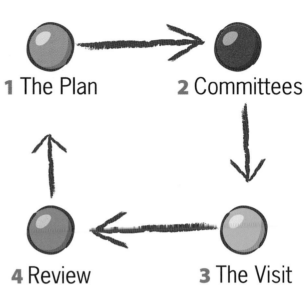

1 The Plan 2 Committees

4 Review 3 The Visit

The plan:

What do we need to find out?
What preparation needs to be done?
Who do we need to help us?
When do we want to do this?

Committees:

What committees do we need to make the process work?
How do we assign students to committees?
What is the responsibility of each committee?

RESEARCH COMMITTEE	PREPARATION COMMITTEE	PERMISSION COMMITTEE
BRIEFING COMMITTEE	WELCOMING COMMITTEE	QUESTIONS COMMITTEE
REFRESHMENTS COMMITTEE	FINANCE COMMITTEE	THANK YOU COMMITTEE

The visit:

A Community Garda visits our class on the arranged date.

The review:

This is a vital part of the process. We need to put a lot of thought into the visit and what the Garda had to say.

At this point we need to ask ourselves questions about the visit:

- What did we find most interesting about what the Garda said?
- Did the Garda give us the information we needed?
- What impression did the Garda make on us?
- Did we understand the points the Garda was making?
- Did we find out at least five pieces of information about the law?
- Do we need to follow up on any issues raised?
- Do we feel the visit was a success?
- Could the visit have been improved upon? How?

Development

Throughout the world people's lives are constantly changing and developing. The speed of this change and development differs from community to community, and from state to state. Change and development generally bring about improvements in people's lives, but not always. Development is usually planned and often only happens when it helps the majority of people in an area. It can be long-term, mid-term or short-term. However, it is also important to realise that development can cause conflict and create problems for communities and states.

Development and the Individual

Change and development are going on around us every day of our lives. Most changes that happen in our own lives, our locality, our country and in the wider world are gradual. For the most part we take very little notice of them.

SHUTTERSTOCK, CAMERAPRESS, PHOTOCALL

However, when we think back to important times in our lives (such as the first day in secondary school, being on a winning team, a birth in the family, for example) most of us can remember the huge change that we experienced at that time. Some people find the idea of change frightening, while others find it exciting and interesting.

Student Task

A Divide into pairs and make a list of some changes that have taken place in the past ten years in:
- Your community
- Your school
- Your local town
- Your county.

B Each pair should then report back to the class about the changes you have found, explaining why you think they have happened.

Often one change causes a series of other changes – this is called development. Many developments are carefully planned with the intention of improving citizens' lives. Can you think of any developments that have taken place in Ireland recently that you feel have **not** helped its citizens?

Student Task

Ask your older neighbours or relatives (parents/grandparents) about changes they have experienced during their lifetime. List them and report back to your class.

Sometimes, the development does not work out as planned and causes more problems than solutions. For example, in some countries that have received international relief following a war or natural disaster, people become dependent on the aid and have not gone on to develop farming and other skills in their own communities.

As citizens, our lives are affected by many developments. A good way of understanding this is to look at the way the role of women has changed over the last century. Changes in their lives resulted in changes in the lives of men and children too. For example, women are as well educated as men now and often have well-paid jobs. This brings more money into the household, allowing for a better standard of living.

Class Discussion

Describe some of the ways in which you feel teenagers' lives have changed over the past 20 years. Focus on the following headings:
1 Education
2 Work
3 Hobbies.

Case Study

Cait's Diary

In rural Ireland in the early 1900s, young girls' lives were far different from nowadays. The following is an extract from the diary of Cait Mulcahy, a 16-year-old girl who lived in a little village near New Ross in Co. Wexford. As you read it try and see how life in Ireland has developed for young women since this diary was written.

March 5, 1906

Peadar Kehoe came by the house today to talk with Daddy. I don't like that man. He must be at least 50 years old and constantly smells of alcohol. I know he came here to discuss me as Daddy immediately sent me to the patch to dig up a drill of potatoes. How I wish that I could go to school but there are very few girls my age who go to school as most of us either have to work at home or work in the Big House in the town.

March 6, 1906

Daddy and two of my brothers have gone to Waterford today to try and sell some potatoes and cheese. Mammy is still very sick and I am very worried about her. She told me that Daddy wants me to marry Mr Kehoe as he thinks I would have a good life. I am not very happy about this.

March 7, 1906

I walked the six miles to New Ross today to sell some eggs and butter that I had churned. I sold very little because most people do not have the money for such things. While I was in the town, I saw many people lining up by the quay to board a large ship which was heading for the United States of America. There were scores of young people about my age from all over the south-east waiting to board the ship. I was jealous of them as they were heading to a better way of life.

March 8, 1906

We got a letter today from my three brothers who are living in Boston. They told us of a great city with many opportunities for young people. Sean and Mike are both working in the city centre on the buildings, while Padraig is working on a large farm south of Boston. They sent some money with the letter which is to be used to buy a passage to Boston for my younger brother Niall.

March 9, 1906

The landlord and his men arrived at our house today and told Daddy that he must pay more rent for the land or else we will be evicted. Poor Mammy is not well and needs a doctor to give her some medicine, but we cannot afford it at the moment. How I wish I could go to Boston and get away from this wretched country.

FIND OUT!

1   List and explain five ways in which women's lives have changed in the past 100 years.
2   Have men's lives changed as a result of the changes in attitudes to women? List and explain five ways.
3   Make a list of the developments that have taken place in young people's lives over the past century. Explain how these changes have been good or bad.
4   How different is life today for a 16-year-old? Compile a diary for a person that age in Ireland today (he or she can be from a rural environment or from a city/town).
5   Make a list of the developments you would like to see take place in young people's lives by the year 2100. Explain your reasons for wanting these developments.

7.1

Design and fill a time capsule with symbols of young people's culture in 21st century Ireland. Include in the time capsule a wish-list for the development of young people's lives by the year 2050. Bury the time capsule in your school grounds (or hide it in a designated place in the school library) and invite the local newspaper to record the event. Keep a copy for class discussion and evaluation.

SKILLS YOU MIGHT USE:
→ Negotiating skills
→ Interviewing young people
→ Designing
→ Hosting
→ Making a phone call
→ Organising

Can you think of other skills you may need to undertake this action?

Development and the Individual

I	M	A	D	L	B	I	T	Q	Q	S	K	B	C	E
R	N	Y	E	S	C	M	P	C	X	C	E	O	D	V
W	F	T	V	H	P	P	E	J	V	G	M	P	Y	I
D	I	A	E	E	M	A	I	N	F	M	A	T	W	T
W	Q	R	L	R	K	C	C	U	U	X	E	U	P	A
H	K	M	O	H	N	T	J	N	E	I	S	I	F	G
C	A	I	P	H	X	A	I	G	C	Q	R	N	K	E
U	H	J	M	O	E	T	T	O	R	E	C	J	D	N
J	U	A	E	A	Y	V	S	I	L	F	O	K	D	F
P	L	A	N	N	E	D	I	I	O	P	E	G	T	Q
K	W	I	T	G	Y	U	E	T	E	N	L	T	D	X
Z	G	M	L	S	E	F	X	C	I	J	A	G	W	Y
W	X	V	O	T	F	A	V	R	L	S	L	L	H	J
M	K	N	Y	T	I	L	A	C	O	L	O	J	S	J
X	V	Q	T	N	V	F	L	K	P	V	D	P	Z	F

- ■ AID
- ■ CHANGE
- ■ COMMUNITY
- ■ DEVELOPMENT
- ■ IMPACT
- ■ INTERNATIONAL
- ■ LOCALITY
- ■ NEGATIVE
- ■ PLANNED
- ■ POSITIVE
- ■ RELIEF
- ■ SOCIETY

Community Development

Communities can develop only if the members of that community work together for the greater good. Every contribution towards community development is valuable, but there are some members who are vital if the community is to grow and develop into a stronger one. These members include:

- Those who protect the community – Gardaí, army, etc.
- Those who coach, teach and care for people – sports coaches, childminders, youth club workers, teachers, etc.
- Those who provide services – fire service, shops, hospitals, banks, post offices, credit union, etc.
- Those who represent the community – councillors, aldermen, politicians, the mayor, etc.

Student Task

1 Make a list of any other people who help communities to develop and state how they do so.

2 Can you identify any groups in your locality who would benefit from community development? Explain how.

Tidy Towns – Encouraging Community Development

Many communities in Ireland have a positive spirit that has helped them prosper and develop. One of the ways in which they do this is by entering the Tidy Towns competition. This competition is a national one organised throughout Ireland each year by the Department of the Environment, Heritage and Local Government. It encourages people to take pride in maintaining their town's heritage by presenting a clean, attractive environment. This makes it more pleasant to live in and more likely to attract visitors.

TidyTowns®
Caring for our environment

The competition has been running in Ireland for over fifty years. Each year more than 700 local communities compete for a cash award and the prestigious title of 'Ireland's Tidiest Town'. When people become involved in the development of their local community, the results usually benefit all members of the community. Schemes such as Tidy Towns rarely have a negative impact on those communities.

Conflict in the Community

Shell to Sea protestors from the Rossport Solidarity Camp in Glengad, Co. Mayo

PHOTOCALL

Development can sometimes cause disagreement between members of a community because not all of them have the same needs and wants. What one person regards as being good for the community may be seen as not so good by another. For example, a local builder may want to knock down an old building and replace it with a new block of apartments, but a local historian may want the old building preserved. Such situations lead to different groups within the community taking sides in a conflict.

WALKING DEBATE

Development is always a good thing.

Case Study

Ballybawn – a Disputed Area

Ballybawn is a two-acre site situated close to the town centre. It is one of the oldest parts of the town, dating back to the Norman era. At present, it is used as a storage depot for the local council, who rent the land from the owner, a local property developer. It is surrounded on two sides by modern housing developments, on a third by an office with 10 car parking spaces, and on the other side is a derelict abbey which fronts on to a main road leading to the town centre. The owner has recently applied for planning permission to build a large four-storey apartment block and multistorey car park on the site. However, not all members of the community are happy with this proposed development and some groups have voiced their concerns to the local planning authority as follows:

The Local Historical Association

'We feel that the proposed development should not be allowed. The area is all that remains of an important part of our historical past dating back to the 13th century. We have seen the plans and believe that a modern development such as this is not in keeping with the area. We are also worried about further possible damage to the abbey. The planning authority should rule against this development and provide funding for the restoration of the abbey and ensure that these two acres are developed as a local historical centre.'

Local Community Association Representatives

'This town has lost most of its green spaces in the recent past. Modern housing developments are popping up all around us. There are no appropriate facilities for our young people. We have been promised recreation areas and a community centre by the council for the past five years – and still we wait. What are our young people to do? We propose that this site be bought by the council and a community centre and playground built on it.'

Local Councillors

'We want what is best for our community. However, we do not believe that this site is appropriate for use as a community centre/play area. People in this area need housing and jobs, and the proposed development will provide both. We feel that it would be better if the community centre and play area were located at another site.'

The Land Owner

'I rented this site to the council for many years at a very good rate. I could have received much more money by renting car parking spaces on the site, but I didn't. I saw it as my contribution to the local community. I now want to sell the site for the best possible price as I wish to retire in the near future.'

Student Task

1 The class could act out a role-play in which members of each group, along with the land owner and possibly other groups that may have an interest (e.g. local business people; local charity for the homeless), make representations to the local planning authority.
2 Discuss some issues that you feel divide your community.

Communities Taking Action

Many communities throughout Ireland have come together and taken various forms of actions in order improve their lives and to develop their communities in a positive way. The following two case studies outline the ways in which a rural and an urban community have tried to make their communities a better place.

Case Study 1

Taking Action in a Rural Community

Developing an Ecovillage

A new community is developing next to an established one in Cloughjordan, Co. Tipperary. It is being developed by people who want to live in a way that has a minimal negative impact on the environment. This type of community is called an **ecovillage**.

The buildings in the ecovillage are designed to reduce harm to the environment. Most buildings have made use of renewable sources of energy and will eventually create enough energy to be able to sell surplus to the ESB.

Cloughjordan ecovillage recycles and composts all of its own waste, putting less pressure on local landfill and recycling facilities. It also has a system to reduce the harmful effects of the wastewater it produces.

A major issue with regular housing developments built over the past ten years has been a lack of space for exercise and enjoyment. The ecovillage has plenty of space for its people. For example, a river walk, a town park and kid zones.

The residents of Cloughjordan ecovillage are aiming to develop a community that makes life a much better experience for themselves and is also friendly towards the environment.

Questions

1 What is the name given to this new type of community?
2 What actions is the community taking to make Cloughjordan a better place to live?
3 List the ways in which the community is minimising its negative impact on the environment.

Case Study 2

Taking Action in an Urban Community

The Ballymun Community Action Programme

Ballymun is an urban area north of Dublin city. It is the site of the largest high-rise public housing complex in Ireland, built in the late 1960s and early 1970s. This was seen as the solution to a severe housing shortage in Dublin at this time. However, families, especially those with young children, found living in a tower block very difficult. Lifts often broke down and there were few places for the children to play. Many felt that there was no sense of community in the area.

Due to a lack of government investment over the last 30 years, Ballymun has degenerated and the community has suffered a wide range of social and economic problems, such as unemployment, population decline, high levels of early school leaving and drug abuse.

To address these problems, the Ballymun Community Action Programme (CAP) was set up in 1990. It is a community resource centre and development programme that is run by people who live or work within that community. The CAP employs a number of full-time staff and believes in collective action by local people to identify their needs and decide on the best solution to their problems. It also supports the work of other community groups in the area by providing support services and training. It also operates a

drop-in centre for local people and other community groups in Ballymun who may want to seek advice or use the services it offers.

The CAP also works to influence the government to improve the situation of people living within the community by lobbying for positive changes in the area. Thanks to this, Dublin Corporation (now Dublin City Council) unveiled plans in 1997 to regenerate the community of Ballymun. Most of the tower blocks have now been demolished and the residents rehoused in low-rise housing. Neighbourhood centres with community facilities have been established, including a leisure centre, student accommodation, a new hotel and renewed shopping areas. A large tree-planting project has also been undertaken. It is hoped that this regeneration will bring a new lease of life to the community of Ballymun.

Questions

1 What problems has the community of Ballymun experienced over the last 30 years?
2 Why was the CAP set up?
3 Briefly describe its work.
4 How has Ballymun CAP made a difference to the lives of people who live within the community?

Developing Communities to Include Everyone

Unfortunately, some members of the community feel left out at times. In particular, people with disabilities are too often judged on their disabilities rather than on their abilities. This is made worse by the fact that many communities do not provide even basic facilities which would make life much easier for people with disabilities and also help them to share their talents within their community.

Student Task

- Make a list of the local community groups in your area which can help people feel that they belong to the community.
- Describe the different needs that the following have in your community:
  - The young
  - The elderly
  - The disabled

Communities can be developed quite easily to cater for all abilities with a little effort on everyone's part. There are four main ways in which this can be done:

→ **The built environment**

→ **Access**

→ **Equality**

→ **Inclusion**

SHUTTERSTOCK 3, PHOTOCALL 2

1 **The built environment**: This means the buildings that people use. With a little thought we can make sure that all buildings in a community are wheelchair accessible.

2 **Access**: Access means making all facilities available to all members of the community, thus ensuring that persons with disabilities can take a full part in it. This could be done, for example, by providing voice-activated computers for those who cannot use their hands, or having menus written in braille for blind people.

3 **Equality**: This means that all members of the community are treated in the same way. For example, disabled persons should be able to go to the same school or clubs as their friends without having to get special treatment because the facilities are not there.

4 **Inclusion**: Inclusion means that everyone can take part in their community and feel that they belong.

Investigate!

Investigate your school or your local community to see how it could be developed to include people with disabilities. Look out for:

- Wheelchair accessibility
- Computer facilities
- Public transport
- Signposts
- Sports facilities
- Access to public buildings
- Anything else that you notice

Questions

Do you think that all developments that have happened in your community in the recent past have been good? Explain your answer.

Examine a development issue in your community that causes conflict or great difference of opinion, and explain how it might be solved using negotiation.

Ideas For Taking Action

7.2

→ Invite a guest speaker from the local planning authority to address your class on local planning and development issues.

→ Arrange for a class visit to the local council or corporation to investigate local development issues.

→ Track an issue in your local newspaper or on your local radio station where a disagreement about a development has taken place. Explore the various arguments involved and have a class debate on the issue.

→ Identify a need-group in your community and suggest ways in which their needs could be met through community development.

→ Invite a guest speaker from a local community action group to find out how they have helped improve the lives of people in the community.

SKILLS YOU MIGHT USE:
→ Letter-writing
→ Questioning
→ Listening
→ Debating
→ Communication
→ Planning

Can you think of other skills you may need to undertake this action?

Regional Development in Ireland

ISSUE TRACKING

Get a copy of your local newspaper and see what developments are taking place in your area.

Not all areas of our country are equally developed. There are great differences to be seen. From the early 1990s until 2008, Ireland's economy grew rapidly. Between 1993 and 2000 it grew by about 70%, but not every part of the country got the full benefit of that. Ireland is divided into two – the wealthy area and the less wealthy area. The wealthy area is mainly that of the **Southern and Eastern Region** (the south and the east of Ireland), while the less wealthy area is known as the **Border, Midlands and West (BMW) Region**.

FIND OUT

1 Contact your local authority and find out what developments are planned for your area in the near future. Why are these developments taking place? What will happen as a result of them?
2 Find out which counties are in the BMW Region.

Differences Between the Regions

The following table summarises the differences between the BMW Region and the Southern and Eastern Region.

BMW REGION	SOUTHERN and EASTERN REGION
Few large towns	Many large towns
Many young people leave the region	Many young people move to this region
One university	Many universities
Main city: Galway – population 50,000	Main city: Dublin – population 1.3 million

As a result of the differences, the BMW Region has been identified as a region that needs extra help to develop. This is called **regional development**. It comes in many forms, including money, jobs, better roads and better communications. The help is given by both the Irish government and the European Union.

However, despite the regional development, there are still many communities in these regions that are experiencing problems. Some rural communities are slowly dying while large urban areas, such as Dublin, are becoming increasingly popular with young people from the rural areas.

Development – the European Union

Many developments that have taken place over the past thirty years in Ireland have been due to its membership of the European Union. For example, new roads and airports have been built with funding from the EU. Much of the money spent on these projects helps poorer areas such as the BMW Region to catch up with the Southern and Eastern Region.

Case Study

Rachel's Story

The following is a story of a young woman who has recently moved from her home in the west of Ireland to live and work in Dublin.

Hi there, My name is Rachel and I am originally from a small village in north Co. Leitrim which has a population of about 80 people. There is a small shop and bar in the village, along with the local church. There are very few young people living in the village or the surrounding area. We no longer have a local football club in the parish as there aren't enough young people to field a team. Most of my friends come from the nearby town, where I attended secondary school.

The local national school closed down three years ago as there were not enough children and the village post office will close next year when the local post mistress retires. Our village has changed in many ways over the past few years and it seems that the village is slowly dying. Unfortunately, I had little choice but to leave. I would like to have stayed in my village, but there are very few jobs in the area, especially in my type of work – computer software development. In Dublin there are many computer companies offering good jobs with excellent conditions and training to people like me. The company with which I now work is American-owned and situated on the outskirts of Dublin. I am renting a room in a house just ten minutes from my place of work. Lots of young men and women from all over the country work in the company. The average age of the employees is 27.

Even though I really miss my village and family, I feel that moving to Dublin has been a very good experience. I have made many new friends and get to go places and do things that I would never have thought possible. I have been at two rugby internationals in Lansdowne Road since arriving in Dublin and I really enjoy going to places such as the theatre and concerts regularly.

Questions

1 Why, do you think, is Rachel's village slowly dying?
2 What effect will it have on the village if more young people like Rachel leave?
3 What important services are at risk when young people leave rural areas?
4 What, do you think, could be done to help the village and surrounding area develop?
5 Why, do you think, do so many young people move to the Dublin area?
6 What problems might be caused in Dublin if too many young people move into the area?
7 Can you list some developments that have happened in Dublin recently as a result of the large numbers of people moving there from other parts of Ireland and from abroad?

Ideas For Taking Action 7.3

→ If you live in a community that is losing/has lost some of its services, organise a petition to encourage the authorities to deal with the problem.

→ If you live in an area that has become overcrowded, and as a result needs more services, produce a booklet that lists the services needed and suggest where they might be located. Submit it to your local authority.

SKILLS YOU MIGHT USE:
→ Organisation
→ Information processing
→ Letter-writing
→ Publishing
→ ICT
→ Surveying

Can you think of other skills you may need to undertake this action?

World Development Issues

FIND OUT

Try to find out why Ireland has become such a developed country. Focus on topics such as education, health and industry. You may be able to get help from your geography or history teachers.

Our world is not a fair world. All nations are not equal, and this can be seen quite clearly when looking at how developed, or underdeveloped, a nation is. Citizens in some countries do not have the same opportunities for education, wealth, health and security that other citizens in other countries do.

Ireland is seen as one of the most developed societies in the world. It is a relatively wealthy nation. However, many other countries are not as lucky and are developing at a very slow pace for various reasons.

Here are some of the reasons for a slow rate of development:
→ Poor health care
→ Unemployment
→ High death rates
→ Poor levels of education
→ Lack of proper food
→ Starvation
→ Malnutrition
→ HIV/AIDS
→ Debt
→ Poverty
→ War
→ Famine
→ Drought
→ Flooding
→ Desertification

Student Task

Choose five of these reasons and explain how each slows down a nation's development.

Facts Affecting Rates of Development

■ Over two billion people in the world are very poor and hungry.
■ Seventy-two million children in the world don't get a chance to go to school.
■ Far too many babies and children die of diseases before their fifth birthdays.
■ Too many mothers in poor countries die giving birth.
■ Often girls and women in poor countries are treated unfairly.
■ Few women in poor countries are involved in government.

Many of the world's developing countries are found on the African continent, and in particular to the south of the Sahara desert in an area known as **sub-Saharan Africa**. Let's look at a selection of these sub-Saharan countries and the problems they face.

Explanation of some of the problems

Debt: It is very difficult for developing countries to improve while they are still repaying loans from rich countries (mostly in the northern hemisphere). The countries of sub-Saharan Africa pay $12 billion each year in repayments.

Poverty: Up to 70% of people in sub-Saharan Africa are living in extreme poverty. They simply cannot afford to buy basic everyday items.

HIV/AIDS: HIV is a virus that attacks the body's immune system. This opens the sufferer to a variety of infections. Only particular medicines can help them. At the end of 2008, 24.1 million people were affected by HIV/AIDS in sub-Saharan Africa, with approximately 75,000 new infections every week. The disease has caused average life expectancy to drop from 64 to 47 years of age in that part of the world. There are millions of AIDS orphans.

How can sub-Saharan nations develop?

The solution to the problems of these countries may be found in the countries of the developed world. **Aid** is the word used to describe the transfer of food, money, skills and technology from developed countries to developing countries. There are many types of aid and it comes from many different sources.

The type of aid that is given to help countries develop is called **development aid**. This is supplied over a period of time to help improve health services, water supply, agriculture and education. Sometimes it is simply given as money, but often it comes in the form of people and essential equipment. The people are agricultural experts, nurses, doctors and teachers, for example, and the essential equipment includes medicines, farming machinery and new technology.

Development aid tries to help the people in countries like those in sub-Saharan Africa to help themselves. The idea is that it is much better to provide training and equipment for the people, rather than send money which may not be put to proper use. Money runs out, while skills remain in the community.

In Ireland there are two main sources for development aid:
- Irish governmental aid
- Non-Governmental Organisations (NGOs).

Fairtrade helps to ensure workers get a fair price for their work and their produce (see chapter 8.4).

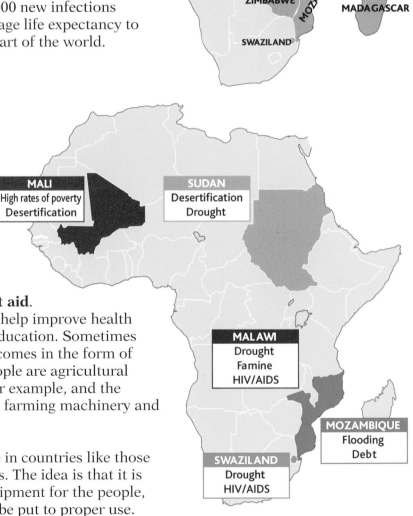

Many developing countries sell products to the developed world but do not get a realistic price for them. We can help by buying products with the Fairtrade Mark. These ensure that producers and workers get a fair price.

Student Task

■ Check your local supermarket or shops for Fairtrade items and list them.

■ Interview a local supermarket or shop manager about Fairtrade products. Find out if they stock them and, if so, list the most popular products and what countries they come from.

Irish Aid

This is the Irish government's aid programme for overseas countries. It helps over ninety of the poorest countries in the world to fight poverty. It is run by the Department of Foreign Affairs. Most of these countries are in Asia and Africa.

Irish Aid helps the governments of developing countries to build and improve hospitals and schools, and to grow food crops so their people can lead better lives. Ireland has nine **partner countries** and gives much needed help to the governments of these countries. These partner countries are:

- Ethiopia
- Uganda
- Tanzania
- Zambia
- Malawi
- Mozambique
- Lesotho
- Timor L'este (East Timor)
- Vietnam

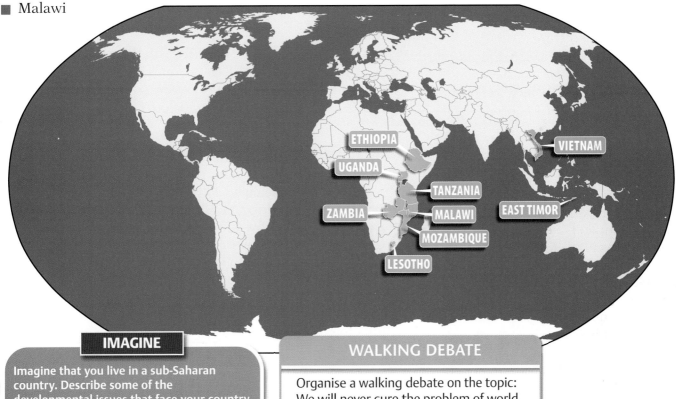

IMAGINE

Imagine that you live in a sub-Saharan country. Describe some of the developmental issues that face your country and suggest ways in which these issues might be resolved.

WALKING DEBATE

Organise a walking debate on the topic: We will never cure the problem of world debt.

ISSUE TRACKING

Check the newspapers, television or any other media sources for news on where aid is currently needed. Discuss these in your next class.

Student Task

Compose a poem or song that highlights the problems faced by children in developing countries.

Non-Governmental Organisations (NGOs)

These are voluntary organisations which have been set up to provide aid to developing countries. Examples of NGOs operating from Ireland are Bóthar, Concern, GOAL and Trócaire.

GOAL – Example of an NGO

GOAL was founded in 1977 by sports journalist John O'Shea. It is an international humanitarian organisation which works to help reduce the suffering of the poorest people in this world. GOAL is currently operational in fifteen countries, implementing relief, rehabilitation and development programmes. Since 1977, GOAL has sent more than 1,100 volunteers and has spent over €300 million in the developing world. GOAL receives funding from a variety of sources including the governments of Ireland, the UK, the USA, the Netherlands, Italy and Sweden. It also receives funding from the EU, the United Nations and the Irish people themselves.

GOAL – Development Aid in Uganda

Some 31% of people in Uganda live on less than one dollar per day. As well as experiencing such poverty, many people in Uganda suffer from the effects of HIV/AIDS and violent conflict in parts of the country.

GOAL's programme in Uganda focuses on:
- assisting street children in the capital Kampala
- providing care and support for those affected and infected by HIV/AIDS in the western part of the country
- implementing an emergency relief programme in the northern part of the country.

Bóthar – Example of an NGO

Bóthar is a third world development agency which provides poverty-stricken families with the means to solve their problems. It does this by giving a family farm animals, such as a dairy cow, dairy goat or a flock of chickens, together with the training and support that they need to look after the animal properly. Milk, meat or eggs not only provide an entire family with a balanced diet, often for the first time, but the surplus can be sold, giving the family an opportunity to earn income. This income allows them to live more comfortably and also to pay for their children's education, which usually isn't free in developing countries.

How does it work?

Established in Ireland in 1991, Bóthar works with a group of partner organisations based in America, the UK, the Netherlands and France. There are Bóthar projects using in-calf dairy heifers in Cameroon, Malawi, Zambia, Albania and Kosovo. It works in conjunction with community leaders who select the most needy families in each area. Once the families are chosen, they are then trained in the correct care of the animal and they must construct appropriate housing for it. When the heifer has been transferred she will calve in the first year. It is an essential part of the scheme that the first-born female calf is donated to another needy family. In time, this second family will make a similar donation and so the gift goes on giving. Once the promise of 'passing the gift' has been honoured, each family may keep any subsequent offspring and build up their herd.

Questions

1 What is Bóthar?
2 How does it help poverty-stricken families?
3 When was Bóthar established?
4 Name three countries where Bóthar has projects in place.
5 Bóthar is an example of an NGO – explain what those three letters stand for.
6 Can you think of any ways in which your class could help an organisation such as Bóthar? Describe what you could do and how you would do it.

Haiti Earthquake 2010

On 12 January 2010 a devastating earthquake hit the tiny country of Haiti on the island of Hispaniola in the Caribbean. The earthquake measured 7.0 on the Richter scale, caused up to 250,000 deaths and 300,000 injuries. Over 1.5 million people were left homeless as a result of the earthquake.

Haiti is an extremely poor country, which at the time of the earthquake owed some of the world's richest countries huge sums of money. It could not cope with the disaster without help from other countries and development agencies.

In response to the disaster, seven of the world's richest nations – the USA, Japan, the UK, France, Italy, Germany and Canada (known as the G7) - agreed to cancel all debt owed to them by the Haitian government. This meant that the money could be put to better use helping people recover from the earthquake.

Non-Governmental Organisations (NGOs) also played a very important role in helping the people of Haiti. Irish organisations such as GOAL were chosen by the UN to distribute large amounts of food, water and other essential items to the homeless citizens of Haiti. Without the help of these NGOs, many more people would have died in the months after the earthquake. These were the first essential steps in the redevelopment of Haiti after the earthquake.

Student Task

Suggest ways in which each of the following could have helped the development of Haiti after the earthquake:
- NGOs
- The UN
- International governments

WALKING DEBATE

NGOs should focus on providing help after natural disasters such as the Haiti earthquake in 2010.

Ideas For Taking Action

7.4

→ Organise a fundraising campaign in your school for one of the NGOs.
→ Find out more about the lives of people in the developing world by inviting a relief worker to visit your school.

SKILLS YOU MIGHT USE:
→ Letter-writing
→ Communication with an agency
→ Listening
→ Hosting
→ Fundraising
→ Planning

Can you think of other skills that you may need to undertake such an action?

Crossword on Development

Complete the crossword below. Use the word bank provided to help you.

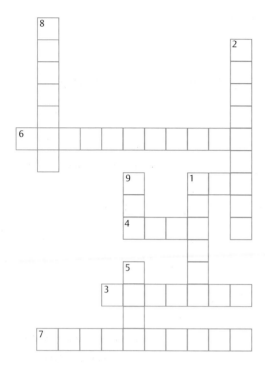

Across

1 The less wealthy region of Ireland.
3 Experienced by people in very poor countries.
4 Countries can get into this when they have to repay massive loans.
6 The process of change.
7 These countries have not fully developed.

Down

1 An Irish NGO which provides livestock to poverty striken families in poor countries.
2 A competition that encourages people to take pride in their communities.
5 An Irish NGO which provides aid to developing countries.
8 These are going on around us everyday.
9 Money and resources given from rich countries to poor countries.

Word bank

→ CHANGES
→ TIDY TOWNS
→ BMW
→ DEVELOPING

→ POVERTY
→ DEBT
→ AID
→ GOAL

→ BOTHAR
→ DEVELOPMENT

Development – Sample Examination Questions

1 Complete each of the following sentences:

(i) Representatives on your local authority are called C_____ .

(ii) Local elections are held every _____ years.

(iii) I_____ means that everyone can take part in their community and feel that they belong.

(iv) The B_____ M_____ and W_____ is a region in Ireland that is poorly developed.

(v) Countries with slow rates of development have very few _____ involved in government.

(vi) GOAL is an example of a N_____ G_____ O_____.

(vii) Three countries that receive help from Irish Aid are U_____, T_____ and L_____.

(viii) The type of aid given to help countries develop is called D_____ Aid.

2 It is proposed that a 17th century castle in your locality be demolished to make way for a development of shops and offices. Your local authority has the power to grant planning permission for the development. You and some other people in your locality do not want to see the castle demolished.

(a) Write down **three** arguments that you would put in a campaign flyer to stop the planned development in your area

(b) Compose an email to your local authority objecting to the proposed development. In your email, suggest **two** other proposals for the castle which would be better for the local community

(c) Name and describe **two** actions that your community could undertake as part of its campaign to save the castle.

Website Watch

Check out the following websites for further information on the concept of development:

www.tidytowns.ie
www.msf.ie
www.goal.ie
www.irishaid.ie
www.fairtrade.ie

www.iro.ie/EU-structural-funds.html
www.bothar.ie
www.trocaire.org/education
www.cso.ie
www.developmenteducation.ie

TAKING ACTION

Raising Awareness of Developing Countries and Fundraising for an NGO

Action projects based on raising awareness of developmental issues and fundraising can be very rewarding and effective. It is important to understand that there are two separate actions here:
1. Raising awareness 2. Fundraising.
It is fine to do just one, but the following is an example of how your class could approach the concept of development by focusing on both actions.

The plan:
What do we need to find out?
What preparation needs to be done?
Who do we need to help us?
When do we want to do this?

Committees:
What committees do we need to make the process work?
How do we assign students to committees?
What is the responsibility of each committee?

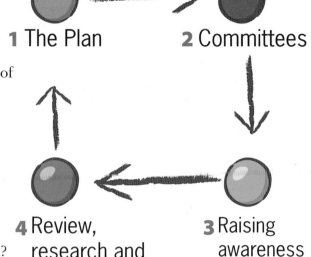

Raising awareness:
The following are some ways in which your class may raise awareness:
- Some members of your class may put on a display of photographs or facts and figures relating to issues affecting developing countries in a prominent area of your school.
- A member of your class may also wish to promote awareness by addressing your school assembly.
- You might like to design a fact sheet on issues affecting development and how students could help developing countries.

Fundraising:
- Decide on a fundraising activity – many Irish NGOs have designated fundraising days in which you may wish to take part.
- Make sure you receive permission from the relevant authorities to collect money (some charities require you to carry a licence).
- Work in close contact with the Finance Committee and ensure all money is properly accounted for.
- Invite the local media when you are presenting the money to the NGO representative.

The review:
The review will help you analyse and find out how successful the projects were. You will need to see the positive and negative results of your work. It is also very important to note the various skills that all members of the class used when undertaking the action. An important step in the review is to write down at least five new pieces of information that you have received.

Interdependence

The idea of **interdependence** is that we are all essentially dependent upon one another. It is impossible for a person to go through life without having to rely or depend on other people. We can all think of a time when this happened, or when someone we know had to rely on us. It is also possible that our actions have an effect on people we may never meet during the course of our lives – people living in the community, in the EU or anywhere in the world.

No-one is an Island

We cannot live our lives without others. We have connections to make and keep during the course of our day.

Ali is a second-year student in Neidín Community School and on the next page he tells us about the connections he made on his first day in the school.

PHOTOCALL, SHUTTERSTOCK

Case Study

Ali's School Connections

When I arrived in Ireland last year from my old country I felt very scared. I did not know anybody and my English was not very good. My father had decided that it would be better for us to live in Ireland as life in our old country was becoming quite dangerous for our family.

On my first day in Neidín Community School, I was really, really nervous. The first person I met was the deputy principal, Mr O'Connor, who was very nice to me and he brought me to my classroom. He introduced me to my classmates and my form teacher, Miss Murphy. Miss Murphy immediately made me feel welcome and asked the other students in the class to tell me a little about themselves and the school. I remember being amazed at how different the boys and girls sounded and looked! Joe, the boy in the seat next to me, told me about the different subjects I would be doing and told me that break times were at 10.45am and 1.00pm. He seemed very kind and friendly.

Sharon, another classmate, gave me a copy of the class timetable and a list of the school books that we would be using during the year. She also told me that the school had a book rental scheme which would be helpful to my family. Paddy told me that the best day in school is Wednesday because the class has two periods of PE and the craic is great. It took me a couple of days to understand what he meant by craic! At break time, I was introduced to our maths teacher, a mad-looking man called Mr Griffin. He told me that I would be very welcome at football training

that evening after school.

After break time, we had two periods of science with Mrs Leahy, a lovely middle-aged lady who again made me feel very welcome. She asked two boys, Paul and Seán, to show me how to do a simple experiment which I really enjoyed and I was so excited that I did not want to leave the laboratory when the bell sounded for the end of class.

At lunch time, four classmates – Marie, Fintan, Brigid and Mike – brought me on an official tour of the school, where I got to see all the various classrooms and was given the necessary information on all the teachers and their reputations. By 2.00pm, I felt as if I had been in the school all my life!

At 4.00pm the bell sounded and in a way I felt a little sad that my first day in Neidín Community School had come to an end. Two of my new classmates – Timmy and Conor – were living quite close to my house and decided to walk home with me. My mother was delighted to see me arriving home with my new friends and seemed almost as excited as I was.

Questions

1 How many connections did Ali make on his first day in school?
2 Describe two of the connections he made with teachers in the school.
3 Give two examples of how Ali was helped by his classmates during the day.
4 Why, do you think, was Ali's mother so happy to see him arrive home with Timmy and Conor?
5 How, do you think, did Ali feel on his second day in school?
6 Do you think that Ali's classmates benefited from having Ali in their class?
7 How would you have helped Ali to settle in on his first day in school?

Group Activity

1 Working in pairs, describe to each other the connections you made on your first day in secondary school.
2 Now explain to your partner how you feel you may have helped another classmate/member of the school community recently.

Student Task

1 Write a brief description of how you think you would feel if you were to move to a new school.
2 What connections would you like to make?
3 How could other people help you?
4 How could you make it easier for them to help you?

The Meitheal Programme

Some schools in Ireland have a system where senior students are chosen to help first-year students settle into their new surroundings. The senior students organise activities to build team spirit among the first-years. They advise them on how to deal with problems they may have during the year. Schools that run the programme find it really helps first-years deal with the big change from primary to secondary school.

Ideas For Taking Action 8.1

Find out how other members of the school community could improve matters for first-year pupils. Present the results of the survey to your student council or to your school's board of management.

SKILLS YOU MIGHT USE:
→ Investigating
→ Listening
→ Communication
→ Survey design
→ Presentation
→ Analysing

Can you think of other skills that you may need to undertake this action?

Cooperation in the Community

Interdependence is essential if our local community is to work effectively. Every day people rely on each other in one way or another.

Questions

1 Can you give any examples of how people rely on each other in your community?
2 Name three groups who rely on others in their community and explain how.

Examples of organisations in most Irish communities that show interdependence in action are the credit union and sports organistions.

1 The credit union

It helps people by giving them loans from money saved by other members. It is not interested in making large profits. It is a service for the members.

2 Sports organisations

Sports organisations also are terrific examples of interdependence in action in the local community. These organisations have many people who help others learn and develop their skills and talents.

Student Task

Can you think of any other organisations in your community that are linked to the concept of interdependence? Make a list of the groups and explain how they are linked together.

Volunteers in the Community

Many people in Ireland volunteer their services free of charge in order to help other members of society. In 2003 the Special Olympics were held in Ireland and its smooth running depended almost entirely on the voluntary efforts of literally thousands of people who gave their time willingly. This was a truly unique event in Ireland.

There are many voluntary groups that help people in our society. Here are some examples:

- St Vincent de Paul – provides charity for needy people
- FLAC – offers free legal information and advice
- Simon Community – gives food and shelter to homeless people
- The Federation for Victim Assistance – supports people who have been victims of crime
- Age Action – helps elderly people in society
- Neighbourhood Watch – keeps communities safe from crime.

Student Task

1 Find out about three of the voluntary groups listed above.
2 Do you know of any other ways in which people volunteer? Explain what it is that these people do.
3 Design a poster which encourages young people to volunteer with a local group.
4 Draw up a list of charities in your locality and think of some ways in which students in your school could help these charities.

GUEST SPEAKER

Invite a local community volunteer to your school to raise awareness about the advantages of volunteering.

Volunteering facts and figures

- Around one third of adults currently volunteer.
- Voluntary work per year is the equivalent of 100,000 full-time workers.
- Some 94% of people believe that voluntary work encourages citizens to become actively involved in society.
- Up to 80% of volunteers are given no training for the work they do.
- Well over 33% of voluntary organisations have fewer volunteers than they need.
- About 60% of young people between 12–24 would like to help the countries of the Third World.

Reasons for Volunteering

→ To help family
→ To be a good citizen
→ To fit in
→ To make a difference
→ To feel good
→ To protect

→ To change
→ To learn
→ To influence
→ To co-operate
→ To repay a debt
→ To act as a role model

→ To have a challenge
→ To feel proud
→ To give back
→ To deal with guilt

Student Task

Rank the above reasons in order from 1–16. Begin with the one that you feel is most important.

Volunteering to Help People in Other Communities

As we saw in an earlier chapter, the Niall Mellon Township Trust is a great example of how ordinary Irish people give their time to help people in another country. Every year these volunteers head to South Africa to build houses for people in impoverished areas. They spend a week working long hours to create a better life for people who are less well off.

The project began in 2002 and by 2008 they had built 11,000 houses. They have built the houses in areas most in need – Western Cape and Gauteng.

The project has become one of co-operation as volunteers from many different countries along with almost 2,000 South African workers now work together. By 2009 it was the largest provider of social housing in South Africa. This shows what the spirit of volunteering can achieve.

Niall Mellon Township Trust

Questions

1 Why is fundraising important for voluntary organisations such as the NMTT?
2 Does this article make you feel like taking action? Why or why not?
3 How does this article link with the concept of interdependence.

PROVERB

When a blind man carries a lame man, both go forward.
– Swedish proverb

PROVERB

Ní neart go cur le chéile -
There is strength in unity.
– Irish proverb

Word search on Interdependence

T	H	F	N	R	P	E	E	B	T	I	D	E	R	C
S	F	A	E	R	V	C	U	T	B	J	N	S	E	Z
I	G	Z	I	Z	E	N	R	Q	A	O	K	I	M	Y
S	S	M	G	N	G	E	R	O	I	N	Z	A	E	C
S	F	M	H	H	A	D	T	N	L	O	O	R	I	J
A	D	N	B	U	G	N	U	N	B	E	S	D	H	E
C	N	K	O	C	K	E	W	I	U	U	N	N	W	W
H	O	M	U	G	V	P	J	F	P	L	A	U	C	B
A	S	T	R	L	S	E	C	P	Z	U	O	F	U	U
L	G	D	H	O	E	D	O	H	W	I	I	V	O	A
L	E	F	O	C	E	R	S	X	K	H	J	F	V	Y
E	R	P	O	A	T	E	V	A	A	R	I	J	N	P
N	P	Q	D	Q	Y	T	U	M	O	D	E	L	U	H
G	S	O	R	G	A	N	I	S	A	T	I	O	N	S
E	I	T	X	N	O	I	T	A	R	E	P	O	O	C

- ■ ASSIST
- ■ CHALLENGE
- ■ COOPERATION
- ■ CREDIT
- ■ DONATE
- ■ FUNDRAISE
- ■ INTERDEPENDENCE
- ■ MODEL
- ■ NEIGHBOURHOOD
- ■ ORGANISATIONS
- ■ ROLE
- ■ SUPPORT
- ■ UNION
- ■ VOLUNTEER

Ideas For Taking Action 8.2

→ Your class could undertake a fundraising event for a local charity.
→ Raise awareness – why not organise an awareness campaign to highlight an important community/school issue?
→ Visit a local senior citizens' centre.

SKILLS YOU MIGHT USE:
→ Communication
→ Organisation
→ Listening
→ Mathematical
→ Questioning
→ Negotiation

Can you think of other skills that you may need to undertake this action?

Interdependence – Ireland, the European Union and the Council of Ministers

The European Union consists of 27 member states with approximately 500 million citizens, all of whom are entitled to call themselves European citizens. Ireland has been a member since 1973.

The European Union is founded on **four treaties**:

- The Treaty establishing the **European Coal and Steel Community** (**ECSC**) which was signed on 18 April 1951 in Paris and which came into force on 23 July 1952 and **expired** on 23 July 2002
- The Treaty establishing the **European Economic Community** (**EEC**) which was signed on 25 March 1957 in Rome and came into force on 1 January 1958
- The Treaty establishing the **European Atomic Energy Community** (**Euratom**) which was signed in Rome along with the EEC Treaty. These two treaties are often referred to as the 'Treaties of Rome'
- The Treaty on **European Union** (**EU**) which was signed in **Maastricht** on 7 February 1992 and came into force on 1 November 1993.

FIND OUT!

1. Name the countries who signed the EEC treaty in 1957.
2. Which other country joined the EEC in 1973?
3. Where is Maastricht?

These four treaties are the basis for everything that the EU does. If the EU wishes to do something that is not covered by one of these treaties, then the treaties need to first of all be changed (**amended**). Examples of such changes have been:

(a) **The Single European Act**, signed in February 1986 and which came into force on 1 July 1987. This amended the EEC Treaty and opened the way for the completion of a single European market.

(b) **The Treaty of Amsterdam** was signed on 2 October 1997 and came into force on 1 May 1999. It changed the EU and EEC treaties.

(c) **The Treaty of Nice** was signed on 26 February 2001 and came into force on 1 February 2003. It changed the other treaties in order for them to work more effectively. It also paved the way for ten new countries to join the EU (Cyprus, Czech Republic, Estonia, Hungary, Latvia, Lithuania, Malta, Poland, Slovakia, Slovenia).

FIND OUT!

Find out the names of the capital cities in the 27 member states.

(d) **The Lisbon Treaty** was rejected by Irish voters in 2008. The treaty was quite complicated and many people did not understand it. The interesting fact is that the people of Ireland had the opportunity to vote in a referendum to accept or reject the treaty while other EU countries left the decision to their own governments. The treaty was again put to the people of Ireland in 2009 and this time the Irish people **ratified** (passed) it.

Making Decisions in Europe

Decisions made at EU level involve five different European institutions:

1 The European Commission
2 The European Parliament
3 The Council of the European Union
4 The European Court of Justice
5 The European Court of Auditors.

The European Commission

The European Commission is a team of twenty-seven Commissioners, including a President, appointed by the member states and the European parliament. They will all have held political positions in their own countries. As members of the Commission they are expected to act in the interests of the EU and not take instructions from their own governments. The European Commission is based in Brussels and has its offices in Luxembourg, although meetings are also held in other member states from time to time.

The main functions of the Commission are to:

1 Propose legislation to the European Parliament and Council – develop new laws.
2 Draw up the European Union budget and submit it to the parliament and the council – think about how money should be spent.
3 Enforce European law – make sure all members of the EU obey the law.
4 Represent the EU on the international stage – meet with leaders or ministers of states not in the EU.

The European Commission proposes new legislation while the Council and Parliament pass the laws.

The European Parliament

The European Parliament is often referred to as 'the voice of the people'. Since 1979, **Members of the European Parliament** (**MEPs**) have been directly elected by the citizens of the country they represent. European Parliamentary elections are held every five years and every EU citizen who is registered as a voter is entitled to vote in them. The Parliament is based in Belgium, France and Luxembourg. The official seat of Parliament is in Strasbourg, while parliamentary committee meetings are held in Brussels. The administrative offices (General Secretariat) of the Parliament are in Luxembourg.

The Parliament has three main functions:

1 The power to **legislate** – it debates proposals for new laws that come from the Commission and votes on whether they should be passed or not.
2 **Supervision** of all EU institutions – it makes sure these institutions are doing what they are supposed to be doing.
3 **Authority** over the EU budget – it monitors EU spending.

FIND OUT!

On a map of Europe, locate Strasbourg and Luxembourg.

Ireland and the European Parliament

■ Ireland has 12 MEPs out of a total of 626. The number of MEPs a country has depends on the size of the country's population.

■ Ireland is divided into four Euro constituencies: East, South, North-West and Dublin.

■ Most MEPs belong to one of seven major political groups. Some prefer to remain unattached.

■ An Irishman, Pat Cox, was President of the European Parliament from 2002–2004. The president's term lasts two and a half years.

Profile of Brian Crowley MEP

Brian Crowley represents the South constituency in the European Parliament. He is a member of the Fianna Fáil party and is linked to a group of MEPs called the Alliance of Liberals and Democrats for Europe (ALDE).

As a member of the European Parliament he is quite busy attending meetings in both Brussels and Strasbourg. One week in every month is spent in Strasbourg drawing up new legislation and voting on it. Two weeks are then spent in Brussels on committee work and the next week is also spent in Brussels at political party meetings.

PHOTOCALL

Brian Crowley's main duties as an MEP are representing the citizens of the EU, voting on the EU budget and making sure money is being spent properly. As an MEP he also helps pass new laws. New EU policies and laws are discussed in twenty committees which specialise on different issues. Brian Crowley is a member of the following committees:

• the Industry, Research and Energy Committee (ITRE),

• the Legal Affairs committee (JURI).

Brian Crowley is also a substitute member of the Delegations for Relations with the United States.

Student Task

1 Contact your local MEP and find out what he or she does.
2 Find out when the next elections to the European Parliament will take place.

EUROPEAN PARLIAMENT
ITS ROLE AND WORK

THE EUROPEAN UNION EXISTS TO SERVE THE INTERESTS OF ITS CITIZENS

Parliament speaks for the citizens when

- EU LAWS ARE BEING MADE
- BUDGETS ARE BEING DECIDED
- POLICIES ARE BEING IMPLEMENTED
- CITIZENS' RIGHTS ARE AT RISK
- NEW CHALLENGES ARISE

EUROPEAN PARLIAMENT OFFICE IN IRELAND

Questions

1 Who published this brochure?
2 Why, do you think, is this office in Ireland?
3 According to this brochure, why does the European Union exist?
4 List three instances when the European Parliament speaks for EU citizens.
5 Imagine that you are a member of the European Parliament. Name an issue that you are concerned about. State why this issue is important and what action you might take to deal with this.

CAMERAPRESS 3

The Council of the European Union
The Council has two parts:
1 The European Council
2 The Council of Ministers.

FIND OUT!

1 The name of the current president of the European Commission.
2 The name of Ireland's current Minister for Foreign Affairs.
3 The names of three heads of other European member states.

The European Council
This consists of:
- Heads of State
- The President of the European Commission
- Foreign Ministers
- A Member of the European Commission.

The Council has a presidency that changes every six months. Ireland held the presidency from July 1996 to January 1997 and January to July 2004. The Council meets twice a year and each meeting takes place in the country holding the presidency. The country holding the presidency also decides on the issues that need to be discussed at these meetings. For example, in 2004 an outline for a European Constitution was agreed during Ireland's presidency.

The Council of Ministers
The Council of Ministers is made up of one minister from each EU country. Which ministers attend these meetings depends on what subjects are on the agenda (up for discussion). If, for example, the Council is to discuss agricultural issues, then the meeting is attended by the Minister for Agriculture from each EU country. The meeting is then known as an 'Agricultural Council'. The Council of Ministers is headed by a President who is rotated every six months and has its offices in Brussels.

The European Court of Justice
The European Court of Justice was set up in 1952 and is the institution responsible for making sure that EU law is enforced. It consists of judges from member states who are appointed for a term of six years. It is also responsible for reaching decisions in disputes that arise:

a) between member states
b) between the EU and its member states
c) between institutions
d) between private individuals and their state.

The court is located in Luxembourg.

The European Court of Auditors

This court was set up in 1977 and looks after the EU's accounts and monetary affairs. Its members are appointed for six years. Its functions include:

1 Making sure all EU money (taxes, etc.) is collected
2 Supervising the EU budget
3 Making sure all accounts are in order
4 Reporting to EU citizens on how their money is spent.

Questions

1 Make a list of the ways in which the EU spends some of its money.
2 Contact the Office of the European Commission in Ireland to find out more about how the EU spends money on projects in Ireland.

Timeline of Important Events in EU history

1957	Treaties of Rome – EEC established with 6 Members: Belgium, France, Federal Republic of Germany, Italy, Luxembourg, The Netherlands
1973	Ireland, Denmark and United Kingdom join the EEC
1973	First direct elections to the European Parliament. Up to this point, MEPs have been nominated by the government of the member states
1987	Single European Act comes into force
1990	Unification of Germany
1992	Treaty of Maastricht – establishes European Monetary Union (EMU)
1995	Austria, Finland and Sweden join the EU
1997	Treaty of Amsterdam – the EU takes on a military role in peace enforcement and peace keeping
1999	Eleven member states launch the euro
2000	Nice Treaty – sets out arrangements for enlargement of the EU
2002	The euro notes and coins come into circulation in most member states
2004	Ten new states join the EU during Ireland's presidency – Cyprus, Czech Republic, Estonia, Hungary, Latvia, Lithuania, Malta, Poland, Slovakia, Slovenia
2007	Romania and Bulgaria join the EU
2008	Ireland rejects the Lisbon Treaty
2009	Ireland ratifies the Lisbon Treaty

The European Union – How It Has Helped Ireland

Cork airport

Kilmore Quay

The NOW programme

PHOTOCALL, SHUTTERSTOCK

- Ireland's roads, railways, ports and airports have been improved thanks to money from Europe
- EU money has provided jobs, education and training for Irish people
- Irish agriculture received approximately €2 billion in subsidies during the 1990s
- Up to 2004 Ireland received €500 million per year from the Cohesion Fund
- Fishing ports have been improved thanks to structural funding
- Irish people can move freely and work without restriction throughout the EU
- Ireland benefits from people and industries from other member states investing in its economy
- The NOW (New Opportunities for Women) programme promotes awareness of equality measures for women – pay scales, maternity leave, etc.

Student Task

Do you know of any projects that have benefited from EU funding in your locality? Make a list of these and report back to your classmates.

Enlargement of the EU in 2004 and 2007 has meant that Ireland now receives less financial help than it used to. Ireland will also be expected to contribute to help poorer countries in the EU acquire and enjoy some of the benefits that we now enjoy. This illustrates just how the EU has helped our country so that now we are in a position to give something back. This is an excellent example of interdependence.

Questions

1 Find out the names of Ireland's MEPs.
2 Which country currently holds the Presidency of the European Council?
3 Who is Ireland's European Commissioner at the moment and what is his/her role?
4 Working in pairs, choose a member state and find out the following about it:

a) State capital
b) Approximate population
c) Official languages
d) Currency
e) The year the state joined the EU

f) National costume
g) National sport/pastime
h) National food
i) National drink
j) Colour/design of national flag

Ideas For Taking Action 8.3

→ Invite your local MEP to visit your class.
→ Organise an EU awareness campaign in your school.
→ Celebrate Europe Day on 9th May. Your class could display information, wear costumes, and provide food from some or all of the member states.

SKILLS YOU MIGHT USE:
→ Letter-writing
→ Hosting
→ Questioning
→ Listening
→ Designing
→ Organising
→ Surveying

Can you think of other skills that you may need to undertake this action?

The Council of Europe

The Council of Europe is completely separate from the EU, even though it co-operates with it. The Council was set up after the Second World War to create a lasting peace and to improve society. It focuses on issues of human rights, the rule of law and basic freedom for all citizens whose countries are members of the Council.

Ireland was one of the founding members on 9th May 1949. There are now 47 members of the Council of Europe, which is based in Strasbourg.

How The Council of Europe Works

The council consists of:

- The Committee of Ministers
- The Parliamentary Assembly
- The Congress of Local and Regional Authorities
- The Secretariat.

Founding members of the Council of Europe

This is how the Council functions:

The Committee of Ministers ⟶ **makes decisions**

The Committee of Ministers makes decisions. It meets twice a year and is made up of the foreign ministers of the member states. However, there are some permanent representatives who meet at least once a month.

The Parliamentary Assembly ⟶ **debates issues**

The Parliamentary Assembly is where debates take place four times a year. It also meets once a year in one of the member states. The assembly has 630 members who are appointed by the national parliaments of the member states. Ireland has four representatives.

The Congress of Local and Regional Authorities ⟶ **develops co-operation**

The Congress has two chambers – the Chamber of Local Authorities and the Chamber of Regions. One of its main aims is to develop co-operation in cross-border regions such as Northern Ireland and the Republic of Ireland, and between different regions in Europe.

The Secretariat ⟶ **daily work**

The Secretariat carries out the day-to-day work of the Council of Europe. It consists of almost 2,000 people working in Strasbourg.

How Does The Council of Europe Affect Us?

The Council passes conventions which are agreements drawn up between states to co-operate in certain areas such as:

■ Human rights
■ Protecting nature
■ Guaranteeing freedom
■ Outlawing torture.

The Council set up the **European Court of Human Rights** to protect people's freedom and human rights. Certain cases are referred to the court by the European **Commission on Human Rights**. The court sits in Strasbourg. There is one judge from each of the 47 member states working for the court.

The council of Europe co-operates with the EU but it is important to realise that they are completely separate organisations.

Some interesting facts on the Council of Europe
■ The Council's anniversary is celebrated on 5th May
■ The Council has played a leading role in the battle for the abolition of the death penalty
■ The Council actively speaks out against discrimination
■ The Council recognises the importance of minority languages.

Student Task

Research the work of the Council of Europe in more detail by going to its website: www.coe.int

Our International Connections

→ **Trade**

→ **Communications**

→ **The media**

→ **Travel and tourism**

Our links and connections with other countries are becoming increasingly stronger in the modern world. This increasing level of interconnectedness is often referred to as **globalisation**.

Our International Trade Connections

Ireland cannot produce everything it needs, therefore it has to rely on other countries to provide these goods. Other countries in turn rely on Ireland for some of their needs. **Trade** is the means by which goods are exchanged between countries.

Food is a basic human need. We depend on other countries for certain foodstuffs that cannot be grown or produced in Ireland, such as:

- Oranges (produced in Spain)
- Tea (produced in Sri Lanka)
- Olives (produced in Greece)

- Pasta (produced in Italy)
- Coffee (from Brazil)
- Wine (from France, among other countries).

Questions	Can you think of five other foodstuffs that are produced or grown in other countries?

Ireland also depends on the other countries for goods such as:

- Oil (Middle East)
- Clothes (India)

- Footwear (Indonesia)
- Electrical appliances (Japan and, increasingly, China).

Questions Can you think of five other goods that are manufactured or produced in other countries?

Transnational Corporations (TNCs)

Transnational corporations are international companies that operate in two or more countries. They are sometimes called **Multi-National Companies** (**MNCs**). Many transnational companies operate in Ireland. Some examples are Pfizer (Cork), Intel (Kildare), Microsoft (Dublin) and Google (Dublin).

Most TNCs have their headquarters in one country, such as the USA, but have their factories all over the world. The energy company BP operates in more than 100 countries worldwide, for example. Some of the best known TNCs are:

- McDonalds
- Coca Cola
- Shell Oil
- Nestlé
- Nike

TNCs are very powerful and control about 70% of world trade and produce 25% of world output. In recent decades, many TNCs have shifted their factory locations from rich, developed countries (where wages are high and labour protection laws exist) to poorer countries (where wages are very low and there is little or no protection for workers). Many factories belonging to TNCs are therefore found in developing countries for these reasons. This contributes towards maximising the profits the TNCs can make.

More Facts About TNCs

- Shell Oil sales are the same size as the economy of South Africa
- Of the world's 100 largest economic entities, 51 are TNCs and 49 are countries
- BP made a profit of €17 billion in 2008 – enough to give every person in India €14. For many people in India, this would be more than two months' wages!
- Just 2% of Nike's marketing budget could double the wages of its workers in Indonesia.

SHUTTERSTOCK

Sport shoes or trainers are an example of goods manufactured by TNCs in developing countries. Look at where your sports shoes were made. Chances are they were made in a developing country, most probably in Asia.

Let's assume your sports shoes cost €100. Where do the proceeds go?

SPORTS SHOES - WHO GETS WHAT?

WORKER	0.40c
LOCAL FACTORY	€11.60
TRANSPORT AND TAX	€5.00
TNC	€33.00
SHOP	€50.00
TOTAL	€100.00

As you can see, the TNC (or brand name company) and the retailer receive the biggest cut from the proceeds. The local factory receives just over 10% of the retail price of the sports shoe. The worker who earns just 40 cent is the real loser in this scenario. Many workers in places such as Indonesia, China and Vietnam earn less than 50 euro a month, barely enough to provide for their basic needs.

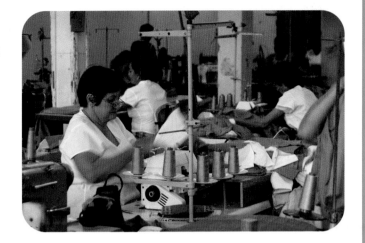

Many workers in these factories not only receive inadequate rates of pay but they must also suffer a range of other injustices:

- Excessive and compulsory overtime. Failure to work overtime often results in the worker being sacked
- Many workers are forbidden from joining a trade union
- Working conditions are poor. Workers often have to work long hours in cramped spaces with little ventilation
- Many workers suffer verbal, emotional and physical abuse from the factory manager. Many workers are threatened or beaten if they do not reach their production targets
- Many factories employ children. Child labour maximises profit for the factory owner as they don't have to pay a child as much as an adult.

Because workers are exploited and have to endure poor working conditions for little pay, these factories are often referred to as **sweatshops**.

Image is important to TNCs that manufacture sportswear. As a result, many employ sports stars to endorse their product. Cristiano Ronaldo, the world-famous footballer, receives a substantial amount of money from Nike to promote its sportswear. It is thought that Ronaldo receives 30 million euro from Nike. Workers producing sportswear for Nike in Indonesia receive approximately 1,000 euro per year. It would take thirty thousand years of hard work in difficult conditions for these workers to earn the same amount as Ronaldo! Think about this the next time you purchase a replica shirt or a pair of trainers.

Questions

1. What is a transnational corporation?
2. List four TNCs that operate in Ireland.
3. Why are TNCs considered powerful?
4. How do TNCs succeed in making huge profits?
5. What are sweatshops?

Unfair Trade – Chocolate Bars

We all love chocolate. It can give us great comfort and satisfaction. It's great isn't it? However, have you ever thought about where this chocolate comes from?

From Ghana to Ireland – how your chocolate is made

1 Cocoa trees, which produce cocoa pods, grow in warm humid places near the equator such as Ghana on the west coast of Africa. The cocoa tree looks quite like an apple tree. It produces cocoa pods all year round, but only around twenty to thirty.

2 Between October and December the pods turn a rich golden colour and are harvested. They are split open by the labourers and the pulp and beans are removed from the husk.

3 The cocoa beans are then put on a layer of banana tree leaves and are covered with more leaves. They are left like this for 5 or 6 days to ferment. This is the stage when the chocolate flavour develops.

4 The wet beans are then dried in the sun, and turned frequently. They must be completely dry or else they will go mouldy.

5 Once properly dry, they are brought to buying stations where they are weighed and put in sacks. The farmers are then paid for the cocoa beans by the chocolate companies.

6 Next stop for the cocoa beans is the processing factory. They are spread on to a conveyor belt and cleaned to get rid of any dust and stones that may be mixed in with them.

7 The beans are then roasted in a big revolving drum called a **continuous roaster.** Once roasted, they are broken into small pieces. The lighter parts of the broken beans are blown away until only the centres of the beans, the **nibs**, are left.

8 The nibs are then ground between steel rollers until they become a chocolate-coloured liquid. This liquid is called **cocoa liquor**. This contains cocoa butter, which is removed, and what is left is a solid block which is then ground into cocoa powder.

9 Some of the cocoa powder is then sent to the chocolate-making factory where it is mixed with cocoa butter and sugar. This creates a dark type of chocolate.

10 The remainder of the cocoa powder is mixed with sugar and fresh, full-fat cream. This mix is dried in a vacuum oven and becomes milk chocolate crumb.

11 This crumb is then finely ground between enormous rollers before extra cocoa butter, vegetable fat and special flavours are added.

12 The milk chocolate is then rolled and pressed and cooled to a certain temperature. Now it is ready to be made into a bar of dairy chocolate or poured over other ingredients to make your favourite brand of chocolate snack.

Chocolate – Sweet or Unfair?

Chocolate may be a sweet treat for us, but it can bring heartbreak and desperation for the thousands of adult and child labourers that pick the cocoa pods and pack the beans. Some chocolate companies in the developed world have been guilty of exploiting the cocoa farmers and workers of developing countries. These people work very long hours in extremely difficult and sometimes unsafe conditions and receive very little money in return. How come?

The chocolate companies realise that by paying very little for the cocoa beans, they will make large profits for themselves. The farmers have to accept these very low prices as they cannot sell the cocoa beans to anyone else. Whatever price you pay for your favourite chocolate bar in Ireland, you can be sure that the cocoa farmers and their labourers receive only a very small fraction of it. This means that the money made from chocolate is unevenly distributed. This is **unfair trade**.

Making Trade Fair

In recent years the **Fairtrade movement** has emerged as a result of unfair trading practices throughout the world. It is not only in the chocolate trade where these practices are evident. Commodities such as rice, cotton, sugar, coffee, tea and bananas have also fallen in price in recent years and are also subject to unfair trading practices.

The prime aim of the Fairtrade movement is to ensure that farmers in the developing world producing these commodities receive a fair price for their goods. With this in mind, Fairtrade labelling has been introduced in a number of countries. Many products now have the **Fairtrade Mark** clearly visible on their packaging. The Fairtrade mark is a guarantee that farmers around the world are given a fair price for their produce. The logo represents the consumer who is celebrating the fact that he or she is making a difference to the lives of farmers by buying Fairtrade products.

Case Study 1

This is the story of a group of farmers in Ghana cooperating to make sure they receive a fair price for their cocoa beans

Kuapa Kokoo (Good Cocoa Farmers Company)

In 1993 these farmers joined together as they knew this was the only way they would receive a fair price for their produce. They set up their own company called Kuapa Kokoo (Good Cocoa Farmers Company). The farmers collect and sell their own cocoa beans as a group rather than as individuals. In this way they can get the best price possible. As well as profits going back to the farmers, money is invested in new machinery, childcare, schools and medicines. A credit union has also been formed for the local community.

Kuapa Kokoo sells approximately 1,000 tonnes of cocoa beans to the European Fairtrade market. This market guarantees $150 extra per tonne of cocoa beans and the farmers can rely on the fact they will be able to sell similar amounts of cocoa beans to this market every year.

In 2007, the Kuapa Kokoo joined with a British company to form a company called Divine Chocolate Ltd. The farmers own 45% of this new chocolate company as well as supplying it with cocoa beans. Divine Fairtrade milk chocolate is available throughout the UK. The members of Kuapa Kokoo now have a say in decisions about how the chocolate is produced and sold. This is a great example of fair trade in action and one that could be repeated in many areas that produce cocoa beans.

Did you know that since July 2009 Cadbury's Fairtrade Dairy Milk Bars have been available in Ireland!

The United Nations (UN)

The aims of the UN are:
1 To keep peace between countries.
2 To help countries develop friendships.
3 To help solve international problems.
4 To help people understand about human rights.

The UN was founded in 1945 after the Second World War to replace the League of Nations, to stop wars between countries and to provide a platform for dialogue. It currently has 192 member states, and consists of many subsidiary organisations to carry out its missions.

The UN is made up of six important units, five of them based in New York and the other in The Hague in The Netherlands:

NEW YORK
General Assembly
Security Council
Economic and Social Council
Trusteeship Council
Secretariat

THE HAGUE
International Court of Justice

The General Assembly

Each member state is represented in the General Assembly in New York. The assembly is like a parliament for all the nations where they discuss the major problems of the world. Each member state has one vote and they make decisions on issues of major importance. Examples of some of these issues are:

■ Admitting new members to the UN
■ International peace
■ International security
■ UN budget
■ Peacekeeping.

The assembly sits in session each year between September and December. However, if emergencies arise it can be called to a special session at other times of the year. It cannot force states to do certain things, but when it recommends that particular steps be taken, it is an important indication of how most states in the world feel about the issue. The recommendations by the General Assembly are called **resolutions**.

Student Task

Imagine that you were asked to address the General Assembly on an important issue of your choice. Write the speech that you would deliver.

The **UN Charter** is a treaty that sets out rules on how countries who sign up should behave, based on its four main aims.

The Security Council

The Security Council is given the main responsibility for safeguarding international peace and security. It is granted this responsibility under the UN Charter. Decisions made by the council must be carried out by all member states. The Security Council has fifteen members – five of whom are permanent, and ten who are elected by the General Assembly for two-year terms. The five permanent members are China, the Russian Federation, the USA, France and the United Kingdom. Ireland was elected to serve a two-year term from January 2001 to December 2002.

The Security Council can only come to a decision if nine of its fifteen members vote 'yes' on an issue. If a permanent member votes no or decides to **veto** (refuses to allow) a decision, then that course of action cannot be taken.

If there appears to be a threat to international peace, the Council will always look at ways to sort out the dispute in a peaceful manner. It might first of all suggest that somebody selected by the Council could try and get both sides to sort out the dispute. If this fails and fighting breaks out, then the Council will encourage a ceasefire. In some situations, the Council will send a peacekeeping force to keep both sides apart. Irish peacekeeping forces have been involved in this on numerous occasions since joining the UN.

In other instances, the Council may impose **economic sanctions** or order an **arms embargo**. In the case of economic sanctions, a country may not be permitted to trade certain goods with other countries. An arms embargo means that the country in question will not be allowed to purchase military materials. In extreme and rare circumstances, the Council may give permission to member states to use whatever means necessary to make sure its decisions are carried out.

FIND OUT!

Name two countries that had sanctions imposed on them by the UN in the recent past.

The Economic and Social Council

The General Assembly has authority over the Economic and Social Council. This Council has 54 members and is elected by the General Assembly every three years. It meets throughout the year and holds a major session in July. Its main job is to discuss major economic, social and humanitarian (people's welfare) issues. It has responsibility for a large amount of the UN's spending on programmes, funds and specialised agencies.

Examples of some the UN's specialised agencies

- **Food and Agriculture Organisation (FAO)**: helps improve agriculture and food security
- **UN Educational, Scientific and Cultural Organisation (UNESCO)**: promotes education for everybody, protection of the world's heritage sites, co-operation in science, and freedom of communication and the press
- **World Health Organisation (WHO)**: looks after programmes which aim to improve world health
- **World Bank Group**: gives loans and help to developing countries
- **International Civil Aviation Authority (ICAA)**: lays down certain standards for the safety, security and efficient running of the air transport industry
- **World Meteorological Organisation (WMO)**: it promotes research on the Earth's atmosphere and on climate change.

The Trusteeship Council

This Council, consisting of seven member states, was set up to help countries that had just received independence after the Second World War. In 1994, the last of these countries to receive this help was Palau, which became the 185th state to join the UN. It has little or no work to do these days, but remains available to meet if necessary.

CAMERAPRESS

The Secretariat

The Secretariat is responsible for the smooth running of the UN. It is instructed by the General Assembly, Security Council and other units of the UN. The Secretary-General provides the Secretariat with guidance on its work. The Secretary-General serves a term of five years and some past Secretaries-General have served two terms.

The Secretariat has many departments and offices, and a staff of approximately 14,000 who come from 170 different countries. Most of the staff work in New York, Geneva, and Vienna, but also in other offices around the world.

What else the UN does:

- Promotes democracy – worldwide
- Promotes development – particularly in Africa and Asia
- Protects the environment – reducing greenhouse emissions
- Ended the government policy of Apartheid in South Africa
- Provides aid to victims of conflict – Iraq
- Helps develop African states – development programmes
- Reduces the effects of natural disasters – Haiti earthquake
- Fights drug abuse – South America
- Promotes workers' rights
- Promotes the rights of children.

Student Task

Divide your class into groups. Each group should research in more detail the work done by one of the EU institutions. Each group should then make a presentation of their findings to the class.

Questions

Find out the following:
1 Who was Taoiseach when Ireland joined the UN?
2 Who is the current Secretary-General of the UN?
3 Who is Ireland's ambassador to the UN?
4 Who are the current elected members of the Security Council?

Ban Ki-moon – Secretary General of the United Nations

Ban Ki-moon (born 13th June 1944) is from South Korea and is the eighth Secretary-General of the United Nations. He was South Korean Minister for Foreign Affairs and Trade before becoming Secretary-General. He spent much of his time as Minister for Foreign Affairs and Trade promoting good relations between South Korea and North Korea. He has actively promoted banning nuclear testing and works tirelessly for the development of peace.

Ireland's Contribution to the UN

Ireland has been an active member of the United Nations since joining in 1955. Many Irish people have worked in New York, The Hague, Vienna and Geneva. However, Ireland's greatest role has been in providing members of our defence forces for UN observing and peacekeeping missions throughout the world. Observing missions means making sure that UN decisions are being carried out. For example, observers are often sent to watch over elections and to make sure new military and police forces are operating correctly.

Peacekeeping means maintaining peace and security by settling conflicts. The peacekeepers in many instances are lightly armed for self-defence and, in some situations, remain totally unarmed. Ireland's first UN mission came in 1958 when fifty officers were appointed as observers with the UN in the Lebanon.

WALKING DEBATE

Irish soldiers should not have to serve with the United Nations.

United Nations High Commissioner for Human Rights

Mary Robinson served as the seventh and first female President of Ireland from 1990 to 1997. She resigned the presidency four months ahead of the end of her term of office to take up the post as the United Nations High Commissioner for human rights. She held this position until 2002. While her resignation as president was a loss to Irish people, many less fortunate people around the world have been helped by her role in the UN.

In 2004, she received Amnesty International's Ambassador of Conscience Award for her work in promoting human rights. In 2009 President Obama of the United States of America awarded her with the Presidential Medal of Freedom for her work in promoting human rights and women's rights.

8.4

1 Invite a member of the defence forces to address your class on the type of work done by UN observers and peacekeepers.
2 Organise an awareness campaign. On UN day, October 24th, your class could raise awareness of the work done by the defence forces on behalf of the UN.

SKILLS YOU MIGHT USE:
→ Issuing an invitation
→ Questioning
→ Listening
→ Recording
→ Hosting
→ Public speaking
→ Surveying

Can you think of other skills that you may need to undertake this action?

Crossword on Interdependence

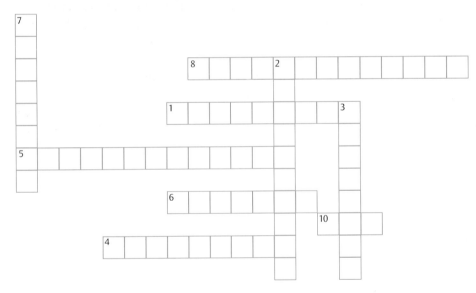

Across
1 Trade that ensures farmers get a fair price for their produce.
4 An individual that gives up their free time to help others.
5 This organisation aims to keep peace between countries.
6 Many Irish soldiers have worked here on peacekeeping missions.
8 These corporations can operate in many countries.
10 Member of the European parliament.

Down
2 The official seat of the European parliament is located here.
3 A union Ireland belongs to.
7 Where the International Court of Justice sits.

Word bank

→ TRANSNATIONAL
→ FAIRTRADE
→ VOLUNTEER

→ EUROPEAN
→ STRASBOURG
→ MEP

→ THE HAGUE
→ UNITED NATIONS
→ LEBANON

Sample Exam Questions - Interdependence

1 Complete each of the following sentences:

(i)   Ireland joined what is now known as the European Union in the year _____.

(ii) In the European Union, legal cases about human rights are heard in the _____.

(iii) The Council of Europe is based in S _____.

(iv) The _____ _____ movement has emerged as a result of unfair trading practices throughout the world.

(v)   The _____ _____ in New York is like a parliament for all the nations where they discuss the major problems of the world.

(vi) The United Nations promotes d _____ worldwide

(vii) The Security Council has _____ members, five of whom are permanent.

(viii)Two permanent members of the Security Council are F _____ and C _____.

**2 In 1985, the 9th of May was chosen by the EU as the date on which to celebrate Europe Day.
Your CSPE class has decided to celebrate Europe Day as part of your learning about interdependence.**

(i)   Write a short speech for a school assembly explaining your Europe Day programme of celebration. You should include a description of **THREE** different activities which everyone can take part in so as to learn more about the European Union.

(ii) Apart from making a speech at the school assembly, describe **TWO** ways in which your class could raise awareness about your Europe Day celebrations.

(iii) Name and explain **TWO** skills that you and your classmates would use while raising awareness about your Europe Day celebrations.

Website Watch
Check out the following websites for further information on the concept of Interdependence:

www.creditunion.ie
www.fairtrade.ie
www.irishaid.gov.ie
www.eumatters.eu
www.un.org
www.coe.int

www.volunteeringireland.com
www.maketradefair.com
www.undp.org
http://europa.eu
www.briancrowleymep.ie

TAKING ACTION

An Awareness Campaign

Raising awareness of our EU partners on Europe Day

This is an interesting and fun way to take action. Europe Day is 9th May and is a celebration your class can join in. By celebrating Europe Day you can create awareness of our EU partners among your school community. The key to organising a successful celebration of Europe Day lies in planning. The best way to ensure it all runs smoothly is to agree on a plan of action and divide the class into a number of committees.

To celebrate the day your class could choose ten (or any number) of EU countries and arrange a stand for each country to display items such as the national flag; national symbols; map of the country; national food; national dress etc. It is up to you to decide what is displayed. The day could be celebrated by the whole school community by arranging for the display to take place in an area of the school that everyone could visit, e.g. gym hall.

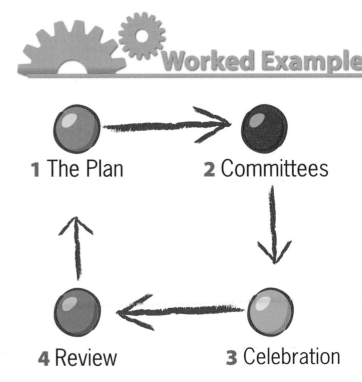

Worked Example

1 The Plan

2 Committees

3 Celebration

4 Review

The Plan:

Which countries will we choose?
What preparations do we need to make?
Who will help us?
Where will we have our display?
Will we survey the pupils who visit the display to find out how much they know about Europe?

Committees:

What committees do we need to make the process work?
How do we assign students to committees?
What is the responsibility of each committee?

PERMISSION COMMITTEE

PUBLIC RELATIONS COMMITTEE

COUNTRY COMMITTEE

PREPARATION COMMITTEE

CLEAN-UP COMMITTEE

SURVEY COMMITTEE

Can you think of any other committees you might need for this action?

The celebration:

Europe Day – 9th May.

The review:

It is very important to review the day and find out what you learned from the experience and maybe how you might have improved on the celebration. For example, your class could ask themselves the following questions:

- Did we have fun?
- Could we recommend this type of action to other CSPE students?
- Did we learn five new pieces of information about our EU neighbours?
- Did other students in the school find out new information about the EU?
- Do we need to follow up on any issues raised by visiting students?
- Do we feel the day was a success?
- Could the day have been improved upon? How?

Assessment

Civic, Social and Political Education is assessed in two ways:
1. A written examination during the Junior Certificate Examination in June (80 marks – 40%)
2. Submission of a Report on an Action Project (RAP) (120 marks – 60%)
   Or
   Submission of a Course Work Assessment Book (CWAB)

This work is usually completed and submitted during the first week of May. You must therefore plan to get your action done well in advance of May to give yourself plenty of time to write up your report/assessment book.

When taking action you should do so in the following manner:

1. Find an issue that is relevant to the concept you are studying.
2. Think about the committees that you may need and form them.
3. Each committee will have specific tasks to do. Make sure that its members know exactly what they are to do.
4. Carry out the action. Record all the tasks and list the skills used while doing it.
5. Evaluate the action – how did it go? What did you find out? Was it worthwhile? What did you learn?
6. Report on the action by RAP or CWAB.

REMEMBER!

- Your Action Project must be based on one or more of the seven concepts.
- It must involve action! It is not a piece of research based on facts and figures from a book or website.
- You must engage with others.
- You must reflect on it and assess how successful it was.
- The Action Project should improve your knowledge of the issue.
- You must write up your own report.

It is a good idea to have a section in your copybook where you can record all the things that you, your committee and class does during the Action Project. The following is a suggestion of how to organise your notes:

WHAT OUR CLASS WILL DO
The task: _____
Which committees are responsible? _____
What needs to be done? _____
Date: _____

WHAT MY COMMITTEE WILL DO
The task: _____
Who will do it? _____
What needs to be done? _____
Date: _____

WHAT I WILL DO
My jobs: _____
What do I need to do them? _____
Who can help me? _____
Date: _____

THE REPORT ON THE ACTION PROJECT – (RAP)

SECTION 1: The Title of my Action Project

The title must refer to:

1 The type of action undertaken.

2 The subject of the action.

You must then tick a box which describes the type of action you carried out.

Worked Example

The title of my action project:
Our class visit to the Garda Training College

Please tick ✓ the type/s of actions that was/were undertaken as part of the Action Project:

Visit: ✓

SECTION 2: Introduction

In this section you are asked to show which concept or concepts you were studying when undertaking the action. You are provided with a box for each concept. You must tick one or more of these boxes. You must then explain how your Action Project was based on this concept/these concepts.

NB. If your Action Project was based on more than one concept, you must tick the relevant concepts and then explain how it was based on each concept in turn.

You also need to state the purpose of the Action Project and explain why you decided on this particular Action Project.

Worked Example
(a) Please tick ✓ the concept(s) on which your Action Project was based:

Law: ✓

Explain how your Action Project was based on one of these concepts:

The Garda Síochána is the body responsible for making sure laws are obeyed. They train in how to enforce the law at the Garda Training College, Templemore, Co. Tipperary.

(b) Give one reason why you chose this Action Project:

While studying the concept of law, the class became very interested in the role of the Gardaí. We thought it would be a good idea to try and find out more about what it is the Gardaí do and how they train to do it.

SECTION 3: Communication

This section requires you to do two things:

(a) Show who you communicated with during the Action Project. You must also explain why you communicated with these people.

You may have communicated with different people during the course of the Action Project, therefore you may need to tick more than one box. However, if you do tick more than one box then you may have to give more than one explanation. If there is no box for the people with whom you communicated, then where it says 'other', explain who they were.

(b) List and briefly explain the main tasks/activities undertaken by the class as part of the Action Project.

Here you will need to list the names of each of the committees. Then you should describe in two or three sentences what it is each committee did.

(c) You will need to give a detailed account of one specific task/activity which you did as part of one of the committees.

(d) You will need to describe how you used two skills during your work with your committee. You must name the skills and explain how you used both.

Worked Example
(a) Please tick ✓ the people you communicated with in the course of your Action Project:

Person/people in the community   ✓

Individuals/organisations involved in this issue   ✓

Explain why one of these people was communicated with and why they were involved in the Action Project:

We contacted Sergeant Murphy at the Garda Training College who told us that she would be delighted to have our class visit the college. Sergeant Murphy deals with all groups who wish to visit.

(b) Write a list and brief description of the main tasks/activities undertaken as part of the Action Project:

The class made out a list of all the jobs and tasks that needed to be done during the Action Project. We felt the best way to do this was by dividing the class into committees. We had six committees and each had their own jobs/tasks to do.

I. The Contact Committee
This committee contacted the local Community Garda – Garda O'Sullivan – who gave the members a name of a contact in the Garda college. They then phoned the Garda College and spoke with Sergeant Murphy. They arranged a date for the visit with Sergeant Murphy – March 7th. It was also their job to meet Sergeant Murphy on the day and introduce her to the class.

II. The Permission Committee
It was necessary to get permission from the school principal to go on the trip to Templemore. This committee did this by writing a letter to the principal, outlining our reasons for the trip and giving him the date and time of the trip.

III. The Organising Committee
This committee had responsibility for booking a bus to bring us to Templemore. Its members had to ring several different bus companies and eventually booked the company that gave the best price for the trip. They had to use the school fax machine with school headed paper signed by our CSPE teacher to book the bus.

191

IV. The Finance Committee

We decided to make a presentation to Sergeant Murphy at the end of the visit. The class decided to present her with some chocolates and flowers. In order to do this, we needed to collect €2 from each student. Each student also had to pay towards the cost of bus hire. It was the finance committee's responsibility to collect the money to buy the gifts and pay the bus driver.

V. The Questions Committee

This committee got everyone in the class to think up some questions to ask on the day. Its members picked out ten questions and each member of the committee asked Sergeant Murphy and the trainee Gardaí two questions each. They also wrote down the answers so we all could remember them.

VI. The Thank-you Committee

This committee publicly thanked Sergeant Murphy and the trainee Gardaí for their hospitality – especially for the lovely lunch in the canteen! A week after our visit, the committee also sent an official thank you letter.

(c) Give a detailed account of ONE particular task/activity from the list in section (b) that YOU undertook as part of the Action Project:

I was a member of the Questions Committee. We met several times to discuss the types of questions that would be appropriate to ask on the day of the trip. I researched and came up with five questions to ask. Each of the other members of the committee did the same.

We than debated among ourselves which questions were the best. We selected six questions to be asked by three members of the committee. I was chosen to ask two questions. I practised asking these questions in front of the committee and the whole class. The teacher listened to the questions and gave me some help in phrasing them. I listened to her advice and wrote up the questions in preparation for the big day!

The two questions I asked the trainees and Sergeant Murphy were:
(1) Why did you decide to become a Garda?
(2) What is the most difficult part of training to be a Garda?

(d) Describe how you applied two skills when undertaking the activity described in part (c) above.

By asking the Gardaí two questions on the day of the visit, I used the following two skills:

Skill 1: Public Speaking

I had to ask the two questions in a lecture theatre in front of my classmates, Sergeant Murphy and six trainees. As the lecture theatre was quite large, I had to use a microphone. This was the first time that I had to do something like this and I was very nervous. It was a difficult thing to do but I was glad that I did it.

Skill 2: Recording Information

As well as asking the two questions, I had to record the answers given. When the Gardaí answered my questions, I listened very carefully and made a note of the key words in their answers which I wrote down in my copybook. When the questions and answers session finished, I then wrote out in detail the answers given by the Gardaí. I gave this information out to the rest of the class when we had our next CSPE lesson.

SECTION 4: Summary of Information

In this section you must give five facts. A fact is something that helps develop your understanding of the concept. Appropriate ones could be things such as:

■ Valid facts which relate to the subject of your Action Project
■ An explanation of a term related to the subject of your Action Project
■ The results of a survey – these could be statistics
■ An illustration of a fact – could be a pie-chart/bar graph.

The most important thing to remember is that you must refer to the **subject** of the Action Project, not the things you/your committee/your class did.

Worked Example
Give five facts that you found out about the subject of the Action Project:
■ I found out that the trainees spend two years training. During training they spend two different periods of time training 'on the job' in Garda stations throughout the country.

■ I discovered that the term 'Garda Síochána' means Guardians of the Peace. Their role is to improve the safety and security of citizens, the state and its institutions.

■ I learned that the Minister for Justice and Law Reform has political responsibility for the Garda Síochána. The head of the force is the Commissioner who is appointed for a seven-year term.

■ I discovered that the Garda Síochána was set up in 1922 as an unarmed force, and it still is to this day. However, in some situations, some Gardaí with special training carry arms.

■ I found out that there are different sections of the force. For example, there is a Rapid Response Unit which is called on in very dangerous and violent cases. This section is highly trained in the use of firearms.

SECTION 5: Reflections
In this section, you need to think back on the Action Project – on what you did and how you felt during it. You should give three thoughts/feelings on the experience and three reasons for them.

A good way of doing this is by using the following structure for each of the three:

I think ... because ...

Worked Example

Think back on your Action Project and the experiences you had while doing it. Give your OWN thoughts on these and explain why YOU think this way.

I really enjoyed our visit to the Garda Training College. I learned a lot about the concept of law and the role of the Gardaí.

I think that the college is a great place to learn more about the role of the Gardaí. I think this because, while we were there, we were brought to see some of the facilities. We saw mock courtrooms, Garda stations, cells and the college's terrific sports facilities. This means that the trainees can train using the most modern equipment available to any police force in Europe.

I think that it is right that most Gardaí do not carry weapons while on duty. The reason I have for this is that there would be more danger of people being killed or injured if they did carry arms. Also, most members of the Gardaí do not want to carry weapons as they believe that it would make their job more dangerous.

I think that all secondary students should either visit the Training College or invite a Community Garda to visit their class. I feel this would be a great idea because young people would get to meet the Gardaí and see what a great job they do and that they are there to protect us all. This would help build a relationship between Gardaí and young people which might reduce the chances of young people getting involved in crime.

THE COURSEWORK ASSESSMENT BOOK – (CWAB)

The CWAB is based on a module of work. What is a module? A module is about 12 to 15 class periods, all of which are based on the same concept/theme/issue. For example, a module of work could be based on the concept of stewardship.

The CWAB is a record of a module of work which includes a report on an action and a description of a number of different classes, all of which are based on the one concept, theme or issue.

Example of a Module of Work

Stewardship – A Module of Work

CLASS 1: Introduction to concept and key words of the module.	CLASS 2: Our school environment – a walk in the school grounds recording the good and the bad by using our eyes, ears and sense of smell.	CLASS 3: How to help our environment – reduce, reuse, recycle, repair.
CLASS 4: A walking debate on 'Sellafield should be shut down now'.	CLASS 5: Write a poem/song or a story on 'Trees – our best friends'.	CLASS 6: Preparing to take action (organising committees and tasks).
CLASS 7: Preparing to take action (organising further tasks).	CLASS 8: Taking action – tree planting and recording the event.	CLASS 9: Evaluating the action.
CLASS 10: Review the module of work and begin to write up the CWAB.	CLASS 11: Continue to write up CWAB.	CLASS 12: Conclude the write-up of CWAB.

COURSE WORK ASSESSMENT BOOK – (CWAB)

Remember that the CWAB is based on a module of work that deals with a topic, a theme, a concept or an area of the CSPE course which you found interesting. You will be reporting on three classes from the module and reporting on an action project.

The CWAB booklet can be filled in at any stage during the three years. It might be a good idea to write up one booklet in either first or second year, and another one in third year. You may then choose the one you feel is the better of the two.

A good tip is to photocopy page three of the booklet and fill it in after every class during the module. This will help you to keep a record of what you did.

Another tip is to use the recording sheets when undertaking the action part of the module.

SECTION 1: Title

The title should clearly indicate what the course work module was about:

Worked Example
Title:
Stewardship

SECTION 2
What my course work module was about:

You will need to write about five different parts of the module of work. One of these can be your Action Project, but you do not have to refer to it.

Worked Example
Our class learned about the dangers to our beautiful environment.
We found out that the policy of reducing, reusing, recycling and repairing helps in a major way to protect our environment.
We had a walking debate about closing down the Sellafield nuclear facility in the UK.
We wrote a poem for our environment called 'Trees – our best friends'.
We organised a tree-planting ceremony in the school grounds.

SECTION 3.1
An account of ONE CLASS I found particularly interesting from this course work module:

In this section you will need to describe one of the classes from your course work module.

Worked Example
(a) The main TOPIC of this class was:
Learning about the many dangers to our environment by using photographs and articles from newspapers.

(b) This is a short DESCRIPTION of what took place during this class:
Our teacher brought in some photographs of environmental pollution and some articles from the newspapers on issues like climate change and CFC gases. We were divided into groups and each group had to choose an article and a photograph and report back to the class on the damage that they showed was being done.

(c) ONE important thing I LEARNED from this class is:
I learned that the main cause of environmental pollution is the burning of fossil fuels. These are things such as oil, coal, peat and natural gas. When they are burned, they release large amounts of CO_2 into the atmosphere.

(d) What made this class particularly INTERESTING for me was:
By researching the articles and reporting back to the class, we were all involved in learning about the reasons for environmental pollution. It was great to be involved in the class. I loved looking at the photographs as I learned a lot from them and I think this way of learning is fun.

SECTION 3.2
An account of a SECOND CLASS I found particularly interesting from this course work module:

In this section you need to describe another class from your course work module that you found very interesting. It is essential that this is a completely different class from the one discussed in Section 3.1 but that it is from the same module of work (in this example it is Stewardship).

Worked Example

(a) The main TOPIC of this class was:
Debating on whether or not the nuclear facility at Sellafield in the UK should be shut down.

(b) This is a short DESCRIPTION of what took place during this class:
Our teacher organised a walking debate on the topic. There were two signs – one at either end of the classroom. One stated 'I AGREE' and the other 'I DISAGREE'. The teacher read out the statement and each student moved towards one or other of the signs. Some students were not sure so they remained in the middle of the room. The teacher then asked us our views.

(c) ONE important thing I LEARNED from this class is:
Nuclear facilities can potentially be incredibly dangerous. One of the students felt very strongly that Sellafield should be shut down because an accident just like that in Chernobyl could possibly happen there and we in Ireland could be in serious danger.

(d) What made this class particularly INTERESTING for me was:
The walking debate is a great way of getting everybody in the class involved in the debate. Even people who are shy and who do not like speaking up can get a chance to show their feelings.

SECTION 3.3
An account of a THIRD CLASS I found particularly interesting from this course work module:

Once again you will need to describe a class from your module of work. It is essential that this is a class that is different from the two other classes that you have previously written about in sections 3.1 and 3.2.

Worked Example

(a) This is a short description of what took place during this class:
The main topic of this class was for students to tell how valuable trees are to the environment and to the people of this planet.

(b) This is a short DESCRIPTION of what took place during this class:
The teacher gave us the following title 'Trees – our best friends'. We were then told to work in pairs and create either a poem or a short drama or a short role play on the title.

(c) ONE important thing I LEARNED from this class is:
Our poem was not very long but it still showed how important we feel trees are to our environment. We were able to use information from our science books to help us understand how trees act as a filter of poisonous gases.

(d) What made this class particularly INTERESTING for me was:
I learned that poetry is a great way to express my feelings on a topic. I read the poem to the class and received a round of applause. The poem was then displayed on the classroom wall. This made me feel proud of our work.

SECTION 4
An account of my Action Project for this course work module:

Section 4 is all about the Action Project that you did as part of the course work module. The Action Project must be clearly related to the module. For example, in our worked example, we have been discussing the concept of Stewardship, therefore the Action Project must be clearly linked to the concept of Stewardship.

Worked Example

4.1 The TITLE of the Action Project I/we did as part of this course work module was:
A Tree Planting Ceremony in our School

4.2 One reason why I/we did this particular Action Project was:
We wanted to raise awareness of the importance of trees to our environment. We also felt that by planting a number of trees in our school grounds, we would be helping the school surroundings to look better and also the trees would help the environment.

4.3 One ACTIVITY that I/we took part in during this Action Project was:
I was in a group that had to contact the local garden centre to get them to sponsor the event. I phoned the manager to see if they would help. After talking to him, he agreed to supply us with a dozen trees. When the trees arrived, everyone helped plant them. I helped plant the first tree by digging the hole for it while other members of my group put in compost and filled in the hole.

4.4 TWO things that I have learned from doing this Action Project:
1. I know that trees are a very important part of our environment. They absorb carbon dioxide and help keep our air clean. We all need to do our best to protect trees from being destroyed.

2. I think that by raising awareness of the importance of trees to our planet other students in our school will have a more positive attitude to trees. I think they will take more interest in our environment as a result of this.

4.5 (a) ONE skill that I used while doing this Action Project:
Issuing an invitation.

(b) A description of how I used this skill in my Action Project:
As we wanted to raise awareness about the importance of trees, the class felt that it would be a good idea to invite members of the local council along with members of the local media to the tree planting ceremony.

I was a member of a committee with responsibility for inviting a journalist and photographer from the local newspaper. I looked up the address of the newspaper in the telephone directory and phoned the newspaper to get the name of a journalist and photographer. Then I typed an official letter of invitation to them and posted it. I received a reply a week later saying they would attend. The day before the ceremony, I rang the journalist to make sure he would be there.

SECTION 5
Something I have to say having completed this course work module.

This section is where you give opinions about the whole module, not just about the Action Project. You are getting a chance to say what you feel about the module.

5.1 One ISSUE that I feel strongly about or found interesting from this course work module is:
I think the policy of reduce, reuse, recycle, repair is something everybody on the planet should take seriously.

5.2 I feel STRONGLY about or found this issue INTERESTING because:
If everybody in Ireland started to reduce, reuse, recycle and repair goods then we would not be creating as much harmful waste and pollution as we do now. If, for example, everybody decided to walk or cycle to school even once a week then we would reduce the amount of fossil fuels being burned in this country.

5.3 What I CAN DO ABOUT IT or what I THINK CAN BE DONE ABOUT IT:
I am going to cycle to school as much as possible from now on. I also think that the government should provide good bicycle lanes in every town and city so more people will be able to cycle instead of using the car.

THE WRITTEN EXAMINATION

In CSPE the written exam is divided into the following three sections:

1. Objective questions
2. Structured questions
3. Open-ended questions/essay-style questions.

SECTION 1 – Open ended questions:

You must answer all questions in this section. It is worth a total of 18 marks.
These are short questions and could include:
■ Multiple choice questions
■ True/false questions
■ Filling in the blanks
■ Ticking in the correct boxes
■ Matching pairs.

SECTION 2 – Structured questions:

■ In this section you must answer three out of four questions. It is worth a total of 42 marks (14 marks per question). In this section you are given a stimulus – a picture, cartoon, newspaper cutting, poster, advertisement, photograph, etc. You will be able to answer some of the questions by examining the stimulus carefully. The answers will be right there in the stimulus! The rest of the questions will be connected in some way to the syllabus but will require you to come up with the answers.

SECTION 3 – Open-ended questions/essay-style questions:

■ This section contains four questions, but you need to answer only one. This section is worth a total of 20 marks. Make sure you select the question that suits you the best! Be careful here as the question may have a number of parts. Make sure you answer all parts. You are often required to put forward arguments or suggest ways of taking action on a topic. Think back to the action you took during the CSPE course – you may find the solution there.